Contei

PART ONE: TECHNIQUES

On Singing Onstage

The New and Completely Revised Edition

David Craig

THEATRE BOOK PUBLISHERS
211 West 71 St. New York, N.Y. 10023

Library of Congress Cataloging-in-Publication Data

Craig, David.
    On singing onstage / David Craig. — New and completely rev. ed.
        p.   cm.
    ISBN 1-55783-043-6
    1. Singing—Instruction and study. 2. Musical theater—
Instruction and study. I. Title.
MT820.C788   1990
782.1'414'07—dc20   89-18671
                                                              CIP
                                                              MN

Applause Theatre Book Publishers
211 West 71st Street
New York, NY 10023
(212) 595-4735

First Applause Printing, 1990

Quality printing and binding by:
Haddon Craftsmen
1001 Wyoming Ave.
Scranton, PA 18509 USA

To my wife,
who taught me that theater,
like comedy,
is no laughing matter

Acknowledgments

I should like to express my gratitude to Gary Carver, my pianist and good friend, without whom my teaching would function without a right arm; to Henry Polic II, who granted me the use of his creative technical work; to Leonard Gershe, whose aid opened the door to Irving Berlin; and to all those who, through the years, helped to shape the work described within these covers.

Foreword

by Lee Grant

David Craig observes in his first chapter that the American actor is addicted to teachers. All of our lives, at all stages of our careers, we explore new disciplines simply to learn new crafts as the necessity to work confronts us. What if, God forbid, you were offered a musical and couldn't sing?

Like eternal children we are forever being tutored for Great Examinations and Great Expectations, trying to mold ourselves into whatever it is "they" want us to be. When my husband, Joey, was a dancer, he wrote on his résumé that his height was 5'9" to 6'2"—whatever it is "they" want us to be.

I first heard of David's classes when we were in that period on Broadway when musicals were "in" and plays were "out." Dramas were opening and closing out of town. I couldn't work yet in television or film because of the Blacklist. I had to be able to sing in order to stay in a shrinking profession. My previous singing experiences had been traumatic and I was earning my own living by teaching acting. I entered David's class with fear and caution.

In his Introductory Class, for purposes of demonstration, David had graduate students perform. I cannot tell you what it is like to see an ordinary actor, an ordinary extraordinary actor, perform after working with David. The mystery of it! Why is she doing that? How sure she is of herself! Why is she looking there? Now there? And the singing seems to take care of itself—the voice follows the thoughts. The concentration is not on the voice! A person in total command is on the stage, an elegant, interesting person who is telling me something through a song I'd heard a hundred clichéd times before, but telling me in a way I'd never heard or seen before. My fear left as I felt a pure hunger to be able to do that thing myself—that particular hunger that makes one want to act, to create, in the first place.

There is a great psychological difference between actors and entertainers. Actors need a situation, a play, and other characters to buffer them from the audience. The actor works for solitude in public, creating an area the audience shouldn't enter, where we are free to create and re-create life. We feel impossibly exposed and uncertain in an entertaining posture. David Craig recognizes this dichotomy and, using the actor's tools, shows us the way to create our own privacy and invent characters we need while we are doing this monologue called song. His approach is unique, image-breaking. For those of us who were still terrified of singing, his class was the Second Coming.

The fact is, I was so enamored of David's classes that I haunted them. I attended his sessions three seasons in a row until he gently pried my fingers loose from my chair and told me it was time to go out in the world. I think he was wrong. If I could, I'd be there still.

As you come to know David through his book, you will treasure him as I do. He is not a teacher who encourages mystery. The mystery is one's talent. It exists or it doesn't. He is a master at creating exercises and tasks that release that talent, tasks that are measurable, that he can estimate you have carried out or have not carried out.

His work is taxing and inventive, and so is he—caustic when you are self-indulgent, loving when you achieve—a Papa-bird training and protecting the faint of heart until the day he pushes you to stand on your wobbly legs to fly.

David is also a snob in the very best sense. He brings to all his students a fierce conviction about who is a talent and who is not. When he works himself up about it it's a terrible beauty, and pure oxygen to me because he cares. He maintains a highly rigid set of values and is so charming and witty that, even when I don't agree with him, I laugh.

When you've read a book you've cherished and reluctantly turned the last page, it's good to call a friend and say, "You're so lucky you haven't read this—it's all ahead of you."

It's all ahead of you.

Preface

In 1978, in the preface to the first edition of *On Singing Onstage,* I wrote that the musical theater was in a "...demonstrably sorry state of sterility" while "the legitimate theater of comedy and drama presents a healthy and vital picture." In the final pages of the volume, I offered the suggestion that "regional theaters would appear to be a fertile breeding ground for tomorrow's musicals." More than a decade later the first quote is true but in the reverse while the prophetic prescription for the ailing Broadway musical theater of the seventies has become almost standard practice, viz., *Big River, Into the Woods,* and the West End of London, if one perceives it as an extreme outpost of regionalism. All may not be well with the American musical but, in the words of Ira Gershwin, "things are looking up." And although ticket prices rise with promises of still further increases, the undaunted public pays with no apparent resistance. In a *New York Times* interview dated September 7, 1987, Rocco Landesman, President of Jujamcyn Theater Group remarked that "...the $47.50 we're charging now isn't really enough. I think ticket prices are going to have to go up, unfortunately, to reflect increases in costs." By 1989, the prophesy had become a reality. The top-priced ticket for *Jerome Robbins' Broadway* soared to an all-time high of $60. The Broadway theater, now more than ever, has become exclusive in the sense that its price tag marks it as select and bars those who cannot afford to attend. There is a small faction of producers working to bring down spiraling costs (and in some instances they are successful), but the established methods of production and profit-sharing are still entrenched procedures, and as long as they prevail it will not be long before today's five-million-dollar musical becomes tomorrow's bargain. Just as the general audience's appetite for a hit musical remains constant, the numbers of young performers who act, sing, and dance and want the world to know it has not diminished. For obvious reasons, this is both heartwarming and disheartening.

After forty years of teaching, I have concluded that everybody sings—those who can and do it, and those who cannot and do it anyway. Some people sing for money and some sing for themselves in closets, bathrooms, and in their cars as they drive. The thing is: Everybody sings. It is of no small interest to observe that doing it in public is not accomplished without enduring some degree of pain. Most people find it disorienting at best and, in extreme cases, self-annihilative. And yet...and yet...why are so many unable and even unwilling to resist the temptation to do it? Is it some atavistic impulse that compels us to use our bodies as instruments that quite literally make music? Or is it something we begin to imitate when, as babes, we are sung to and sung at—something that inevitably induces us to sing out? Furthermore, everybody who wants to sing for money yearns to sing with evident know-how and personal style. These elements that, in the long ago, identified the unique individuality of a performer were honed in theaters, on vaudeville stages, and in nightclubs. Today, vaudeville, even as a word in our vocabulary, is long gone, and nightclubs either present stand-up comedians exclusively or showcase singers who perform their "acts" before friends whose presence they are responsible for. By virtue of the entire world's abiding affection for it, the musical theater remains the sole venue in which the actor/singer/dancer can work.

With almost no place to turn for training "by doing," the phenomenon of study has established itself as the sole available method for learning stage techniques. Today one can attend colleges and universities where, as well as receiving a degree, an undergraduate can major in drama and/or musical theater. The expertise of the faculties is not always expert and, in the case of the lyric theater, an efficient pedagogy is yet to be defined. At this moment in time, the marketplace is in no way threatened by academia. An actor, a dancer, or a singer, intent upon a career in the musical theater, must inevitably seek out truly professional instruction. This search for and choice of teachers can be daunting to the young performer confronted with the number of teachers at work in New York and Los Angeles—and points between. There is, for the hiring, an accredited first echelon of established acting, singing, and dancing instructors, but added to their ranks are singing teachers who coach and coaches who will add a dollop of vocal technique to an hour of "Give me more on the word *love*"; there are acting teachers who will edit an actor's singing performance; and there are dance teachers who operate quasigymnasia where actors can keep in shape while conquering a plié, a time-step, and a waltz-clog. The ascension of teachers has redounded to their advantage and they enjoy a distinct cachet. The performer's biography in a playbill and on a résumé, which once listed only work credits, now informs the audience and the hirer of the names of those with whom the performer has studied and furnishes a kind of presumptive validation.

It was inevitable that the hunger for study would breed addiction. Today, young people appear to have added to the need to learn, the illusion that study fills the void created by unemployment. They quite literally "collect" teachers, impoverishing themselves in order to feed their habit. I am not speaking here to the beginner. Now, more than ever, musical theater suffers from a bad case of amateuritis. The techniques and craft of the art of performing are acquireable and should be respected enough to be learned, but one fact cannot be denied: Any one teacher's concept of "how to" can be, and often is, a "how *not* to" under the roof of another school of thought. I exempt the "workshop" from the notion that open-ended study can result in diminished returns. From my observation of its function, it furnishes a hall in which a body of professionals, chosen by an elected slate of officers, performs plays, scenes, and exercises. In actuality it can be educative, but the experience is proctored, not tutored, by peers.

Let me attempt further to define this somewhat unfashionable theory. When a beginner wants to learn how to do something, he or she searches for the teacher who teaches the subject. From the start, their roles are clearly defined. When the student has learned to perform what he or she originally asked of the teacher, those roles become blurred. No longer is it a question of how to *do* the work, but rather what the teacher *thinks* of it. In the study of the creative and interpretive arts those judgments, necessarily subjective, can be dangerous. A teacher's opinion, regardless of its accreditation, is still a personal opinion and, by virtue of that fact, arguable. Further, an open-ended dependency on a teacher(s) contains lethal power: It can atrophy an artist's sense of self-criticism. While the judgments made by an agent, a hirer, or an audience may be just as contestable and far more innocent, nevertheless they can influence and even govern a career. Clearly, I do not place dance classes and singing lessons within the context of this argument, since their contribution to the artist's life is to maintain muscles that are required to sustain performance. However, it is important to remember that we study in order to achieve work but it is only through work—whether with good, indifferent, or even bad actors and directors before good, bad, or indifferent audiences—that we learn to assess what we do. Further advice to the neophyte: Attend performances and learn to measure the work you witness. Listen, reject, and even borrow from those you esteem. The late preeminent English director Tyrone Guthrie wrote that "No art is completely original. We all learn, borrow, steal, if you like, from another. But if this is theft, then all are thieves who have the wit to profit from another's experience." (Relative to this advice, George S. Kaufman once said to me that he did not believe one could learn anything about the doing of something in our profession. When I confessed that I was learning a great deal from working with him, he suggested that I was only learning what *not* to do, which was something else again. His words have left an indelible mark, and their effect can be found throughout the technique sections of this book: the *don'ts* always precede the *do's).*

The awful truth is that, much as we try to resist the responsibility, our work is fated always to be assessed by the severest of critics: ourselves. It is our burden and our anguish. The questions remain forever unanswered: Was the work good enough? What could have made it better? What could have been done to make it the best? And what *is* the best? In any learning process, Oscar Hammerstein's "There's a hill beyond a hill beyond a hill beyond a hill..." pertains. How to perform is mastered throughout a lifetime. It begins with the help of a teacher but must take its leave of the studio atmosphere where, no matter the excellence of its verisimilitude to the marketplace, it is not and can never be the place where tickets are bought and sold.

I am reminded of a story, possibly apocryphal, told about the late Ivor Novello, master of English operetta. Throughout the years, during auditions for his shows, a woman would appear among the many aspirants to sing for him. She was inept, but rejection never discouraged her. With every new production, there she was again, older but no better. At last, out of pity and a grudging regard for her persistence, he instructed his stage manager to inform the by now old woman that there would be a job for her in his new musical. Upon hearing the news, however, she refused the offer, confessing that she only liked to audition, and left the theater.

Whenever the need for example or assignment requires a lyric or a song, I have chosen material written for the theater. As the title affirms, singing on a stage requires vocal sound, a lyric of substance, and the diction to articulate it. A song is much like a costume designed to advertise the talent and the appearance of the performer. Either it does this or it doesn't. If it doesn't, a better choice must be made. I do not rule out the contemporary popular music library as a source from which to choose music for auditioning on stages and in rooms, but it is important to remember that current songs tend to live more effectively on recordings with sound tracks that are masterpieces of aural splendor. Deprived of these accompaniments—at an audition there is just a piano, seldom in tune and often inaudible—the songs are apt to betray a melodic, harmonic, and lyric inanity. More to the point, they are most often sung by the composer/lyricist whose untrained voice is better heard up-country than downstage. Even when it has a strong dramatic statement, the song may not indicate for the hirer the performer's vocal highs and lows. Of course, this is patent generalization, and there are many exceptions that are stageworthy and, in certain works, more germane to the piece for which the auditions are being held. But there is another, more important, motive for staying with music written for the theater in the technical sections of this volume: Unlike the ephemeral hit tune, theater music remains published, available in sheet music and in vocal selections and collections.

I do not pretend to be happy teaching material that, too often, may live in a time warp. On occasion the lyrics of a show tune are inimical to the sociosexual and racial changes that have occurred in America, and I am impelled to make discreet alterations or banish the song from the current repertoire. Today's woman would not willingly sing

> What's the difference if I say I'll go away
> When I know I'll come back on my knees some day,
> For no matter what he is,
> I am his forever!

> ("My Man" by Maurice Yvain and Channing Pollock, from *The Ziegfeld Follies of 1921*)

nor a black artist accept

> Play that music for me and my sweet
> All dark people is light on their feet
> And just the same as flowers get honey
> All God's chillun got buck and wings
> Pale-face babies don't dance in the street
> All dark people are light on their feet.

> ("All Dark People" by Rodgers and Hart, from *Babes in Arts*, 1937)

nor anyone tolerate

> Each poor man has a wife he must stick to
> Men of fashion can be cocky
> To be caught in flagrante delicto
> Is much too good for the average mockey!

> ("Too Good for the Average Man" by Rodgers and Hart, from *On Your Toes*, 1936)

This lyric was subsequently altered by Mr. Hart to read

Each poor man has a wife he must stick to
Rich men have a diff'rent habit
To be caught in flagrante delicto
Is much too good for the average rabbit.

It is of some interest that my discomfort with this time warp is not shared by those whom I teach. There is a distinct nostalgia for the entire output of the Gershwins, Rodgers and Hart, Cole Porter, Irving Berlin, Kurt Weill, and Harold Arlen and... and... As for the words and music of those who are still alive and well and writing, one has available lavish collections and recordings. The work of Stephen Sondheim, for example, is on sale at the corner music store in an abundance that gives testimony to his appeal to performers and audiences alike.

Much of this book is devoted to an effort to define the undefinable. Words and descriptions are necessities but not always clarifications. Michael Chekhov, in his volume *To the Actor*, remarks:
"...The abstruse nature of the subject [acting] requires not only concentrated reading, not alone clear understanding, but co-operation with the author. For that which could be made easily comprehensible by personal contact and demonstration, must of necessity depend on mere words and intellectual concepts.... Unfortunately, there is no other way to co-operate: the technique of acting can never be understood without practising it."
To this comforting caution I would add that "mere words" create rules with their own exceptions, and that these exceptions, in turn, have *their* validity. But the charting must begin somewhere, and I have chosen as a starting point that place of transition wherein the actor's text (the script of his play) becomes the actor/singer's lyric, which is the script of his song.

This handbook offers a methodology to make less discomforting the terror the actor and the dancer endure when they are asked to sing what they have been previously wont to say. The work has been molded through forty years, filtered down and given its definition by those who have worked with it. For the singer, it may reprise what he or she knows already; discard what has no value for you. In the whole, it is meant to be read by knowledgeable young performers who are about to begin a flirtation with the musical theater. If, in the text, I appear to single out the actor, I am impelled to do so because of his musical innocence. However, the work as described is applicable to a far wider range of readers. A knowledge of music is not required background. The text of the song is everything. If you can hear pitch and rhythm, this book is for you.

There are three divisions in the classes I teach. The First and Second Classes, each between six and eight weeks long, are concerned with the techniques outlined in Part One in the Contents. The·Third, or Performance, Class, is open-ended and its name is self-explanatory. Part Two concerns the elusive craft of performing, and that theme is further investigated in the volume that follows this one: *On Performing*.

Finally, I want to affirm my gratitude to all the actors, dancers, and singers with whom I have worked. It is forty years since I began to attempt a definition of what singing is about for those who had never interpreted anything but spoken text. Since this work has generally been shared with artists well into their careers, I have been fortunate to have taught some of our best American actors and actresses. The calibre of a teacher's work is mirrored in the quality of his students. The high standards achieved and maintained in my classes are the result of their talents and skills. I am in their debt.

Addendum: Rather than drowning in a sea of references to "his" or "her," this volume asks the pronoun "his" to do double-duty. Women readers are asked to forebear and forgive.

PART ONE

Techniques

1

Words as Script

As I understand it, some actors, perhaps most actors, work on the theme first, on the idea first, on what they are. I work on something else. I work on words, nothing but words.

—Paul Muni

The neophyte actor/singer, after the first apprehensive weeks during which he settles for survival and little else, begins to assess the scene. His first complaint concerns the minimal subject matter that finds expression in maximal redundancy. Consider the subject of the chagrin and sorrow that litter the battlefields of the gender wars. They can be wailed in countless variations:

1. "I Love Her (Him) But She (He) Doesn't Love Me," "He (She) Loves Me But I Don't Love Him (Her)," or "Why Doesn't Anybody Love Me?"

2. Beyond love requited and un–, there is the guarantee of pie-in-the-sky times: "What a Day This Has Been But Tomorrow Will Be Lovelier On That Great-Come-And-Get-It Day When You Can See Forever And All Your Fords Will Be Buicks Mañana!"

3. If the promise of prosperity around the corner is not sufficient, didactic instruction on how to be happy is available: ("Get Happy!") for "You Only Have One Life to Live So Why Not Sing All Your Blues Away Because The Devil Is Afraid of Music."

4. Further, if the performer can dance as well as sing, there are lyrics that exhort the listener to "Pick Yourself Up," "Change Partners," and, "Cheek to Cheek," do "The Continental," "The Piccolino," ball the Jack, conga, tango, rhumba, bossa nova, slow dance, soft-shoe, polka, rock 'n' roll and, step by step in "Top Hat, White Tie, and Tails," "Build a Stairway to Paradise."

5. Do you have the blues? You can have them in St. Louis, Memphis, Kansas City, on Beale Street, Basin Street, and on the Blue Danube (" ... When the band is playing the song that keeps them swaying, the Blue Danube Blues"). The same blues can be had " ... In the Night," "In the Wee Small Hours of the Morning," at a " ... quarter to three," on a "Lazy Afternoon," "In the Blue of Evening," or "When the sun comes out and the rain stops beating on your window-pane" in all that "Stormy Weather."

6. Tautological paeans can be sung to Alice, Amy, Angela, Angelina, Bedelia, " ... I want to steal ya"), Caroline, Cecelia, Cinderella (" ... Here's a kiss for ... "), Circe (" ... who showed men no mercy"), Cornelia, Dina, Diana, Dorothea, Edith (" ... she possessed what ev'ry man needeth"), Fred (" ... I'm in love with a girl named ..."), Gertie, Hannah, Irma (" ... she's heaven on terra firma"), Jenny, Laura, a Lady (unnamed, from Spain), Liza, Shanghai Lil, Lili Marlene, Lou, Louise and Louisa, Lorraine, Lucy, Lydia (" ... the tattooed lady"), Mary, Marie, Maria and Marietta, Mona Lisa, Nancy (" ... with the laughing face"), Nina (" ... from Argentina"), Niña (" ... I'll be having neurasthenia till I make you mine!"), Olivia, Ophelia, Peg, Psyche along with Venus and Cleo (" ... her melodies are in my key!"), Rose (who hails from Washington Square), Rosie and Rosabella, Ruby, Rita (" ... nothing sweeta!"), Roxanne, Sadie, Stella, Sylvia (who is she?), Sue (she's sweet), Virginia (" ... the devil's in ya!"), Mrs. Worthington and her daughter (name withheld), Miss Otis and, in package deals, the Sabines (" ... them sobbin' women"), and the Lorelei.

7. Women, on the other hand, are less adulatory when they sing about their men: Jim " ... never sends me pretty flowers"; Bill's " ... form and face are not the kind that you would find in a statue." Some are beastly: "Why Can't You Behave?"; some employ them: "Dinner for One, Please, James"; some are merely "Tom, Dick or Harry," or an anonymous Lamplighter; while others are incompetent: "Sam, You Made the Pants Too Long!" They are heartless: "Most Gentlemen Don't Like Love—They Just Like to Kick It Around!"; faithless: as Johnny was to Frankie; roamers: "Come Home, Joe, Come Home"; or downright stupid: "The Gentleman Is a Dope."

8. You can sing eloquently about: New York, Oklahoma, Iowa, Texas, Tennessee, Carolina, Californi–ay, Missouri, Hawaii, Georgia, Louisiana (both of its "Purchase" and the "Hayrides" therein), Rhode Island, Maine, Vermont, Mississippi, but in all cases the burden of the lyric stays the same—only the title changes.

9. Cities, too, are extollable: New York, New York, including its East Side and its West Side, Broadway, Herald Square, Forty-Second Street, Fifth Avenue, the Bowery, suburban New Rochelle, and Yonkers; Chicago; Hollywood; Miami; New Orleans; and farther afield: Paris; London; Rome; Naples; Capri; Venice; Rio de Janeiro; Ipanema; and a region " ... south of the border down Mexico way."

This listing is abridged, but it offers enough justification for the beginner performer to understand why, early in his singing career, there is a sneaking sensation that he has sung it all before.

As musical theater has matured in the last two decades, lyricists (Sondheim, Harnick, Ebb, among others) have significantly broadened the range of subject matter that can be vocalized. The contemporary popular music scene has been enriched, too, by the work of women who tend to slant the need to love and/or be loved toward the less abject subject of aloneness. Dory Previn's "The Lady with the Braid" is a light year away from the above quoted extract from "My Man."

Would you care to stay till sunrise?
It's completely your decision:
It's just that goin' home is such a ride.
Goin' home is such a ride, goin' home is such a ride
Isn't goin' home a lo-lonely ride?
Would you hang your denim jacket
Near the poster by Picasso?
Do you sleep on the left side or the right? —or the right?
Would you mind if I leave on the light?
Would you mind if it isn't too bright?
Now, I need the window open
So, if you happen to get chilly
There's this coverlet my cousin hand crocheted—hand crocheted
Do you mind if the edges are frayed?

Would you like to unfasten my braid?
Now, I'll make you in the mornin'
A cup of homemade coffee,
I will sweeten it with honey and with cream.
When you sleep do you have dreams?
You can read the early paper
And I can watch you while you shave
Oh God! The mirror's cracked!
When you leave will you come back?
You don't have to answer that at all
The bathroom door is just across the hall
You've got an extra towel on the rack
On the paisley-patterned-paper wall
There's a comb on the shelf
I papered that wall myself—that wall myself.
Would you care to stay till sunrise?
Now it's completely your decision:
It's just the night cuts through me like a knife—like a knife
Would you care to stay awhile and save my life?
Would you care to stay awhile and save my life?
I don't know what made me say that—
I've got this funny sense of humor
You know I could not be downhearted if I tried—if I tried
It's just that goin' home is such a ride
Goin' home is such a ride, goin' home is such a ride
Isn't goin' home a lo-lonely ride?
Isn't goin' home a lo-lonely ride?
Isn't goin' home a lo-lonely ride?

Protest songs have found popular appeal, but in the context of the theater, Bruce Springsteen's pen is far less mighty than Brecht's.

The French chanson, as much concerned with *l'amour* as its American and English counterparts, often offers stunning and substantial subject matter. It is indicative of the variety of Jacques Brel's best work that, long after his death, revue productions of his songs still occur with surprising consistency. Edith Piaf sang the same heartbreakers favored by Helen Morgan at the height of her popularity but, here again, Piaf's song handles are more provocative and theaterworthy. "L'Accordioniste," "Les Cloches," and the extraordinary "Les Blouses Blanches" come to mind.

For the actor accustomed to the multiplicity of published plays available for study-work, the narrow and reiterative range of dramatic statements that can be sung is disheartening. One can only admire the lyricist who is able to create words with just enough english on them to give them the appearance of originality. It is understandable why today's young performers are drawn to the work of Stephen Sondheim, for he alone creates songs whose range of subject matter engages them. He sings of social protest ("Gee, Officer Krupke!" and Sweeney Todd's "Epiphany"), the downside of urban life ("Another Hundred People" and "The Ladies Who Lunch"), middle-age discontent ("The Road You Didn't Take" and "Too Many Mornings"), the artist's tortured credo ("Finishing the Hat"), the intimate conversation between parent and child ("Children and Art"), the pain of connection ("Every Day a Little Death," "Send in the Clowns," and "Agony"), how the making of history is translated into human experience ("Someone in a Tree")—the list is only partial but his voice sustains a relentless commitment to currency even at the expense of commercial appeal.

It must be remembered that in the first half of this century, the songs that Broadway sang achieved national and even international renown. Today's musical scores do not enjoy anything like that popularity. The recording industry is busy wooing the young teenage record buyer, and show albums, few in number as they are, rarely if ever appeal to a wide record-buying public. (On occasion, a popular vocalist will issue an album either totally dedicated to nostalgia or inclusive of an arcane Sondheim song, or there was the 1987 Barbra Streisand album dedicated entirely to his music and lyrics—and in most cases these achieve phenomenal success.) There have been notable exceptions: *My Fair Lady, West Side Story, The Sound of Music,* to name a few, but these are triumphant Broadway hits that toured extensively and were ultimately filmed. Although their scores are known to a large, nonparochial public, I wonder how many among them can tell you who wrote the music and the words.

CATEGORIES OF LYRICS

When an actor auditions for a play, he will be given a scene the director has chosen from the manuscript. He will be able to "read" intelligibly because the material has been given a contextual relevance. Auditions for musicals are guessing games in which the performer's choice of what to sing is based on any scrap of information he can come by. When a theater song is sung out of the context that gave it its life, anything goes that will make it stageworthy. However, no one wants to be told to "do it any way you care to." The great American humorist, Ring Lardner, once said that everything on a stage can be said to " ... take place in Jeopardy." The hirer, just as the audience, must pay attention. You may choose to sing whatever seems apt, but remember that songs have implicitly the power to place you in jeopardy. Let me try to categorize the lyrics and suggest ways that will defend you against even the best of them.

I.   The *Subjective* Lyric.

This group is always easy to identify—"I" and "me" are liberally sprinkled throughout the script. Here, the lyrics of Oscar Hammerstein:

Why was I born? Why am I living?
What do I get? What am I giving?
Why do I want the things I daren't hope for?
What can I hope for?
I wish I knew.
Why do I try to draw you near me?
Why do I cry? You never hear me.
I'm a poor fool but what can I do?
Why was I born to love you?

> ("Why Was I Born?," music and lyrics by Jerome Kern and Oscar Hammerstein II, from *Sweet Adeline*, 1929. Copyright © 1929 T. B. Harms Company. Copyright renewed. All rights reserved including the rights of public performance for profit. International copyright secured. Made in U.S.A. Used by permission.)

This is an interesting, if somewhat stacked, example. The performer is denied even puzzlement to carry the action. The questions are rhetorical; the last line implies that she knew the answer all along. With little push, the singer is lured into a self-pitying whine that deprives the audience of any involvement. Therein lies the jeopardy implicit in the subjective lyric. The rule: *Do not sing it subjectively.* Internalized focus must be shunned and the performance geared to a relentless *objectivizing* of the text. The singer's mouth can be expected to deliver the words as she makes her "intention" clear: to make the listener (the "you") *care* why she (the "I") was born. Today, the image of the gin-soaked chanteuse for whom this kind of song was a trademark is out of style, but the heartbroken archetype has not disappeared, only put away her bottle. Sober, she can be found, still self-absorbed, in Dory Previn's above-quoted "The Girl with the Braid."

II.   The *Objective* Lyric.

Here, the operative word is the ubiquitous *you*. From the pen of Cole Porter (although his editor, Robert Kimball, cannot vouch for it):

> You're the top! You're Miss Pinkham's Tonic
> You're the top! You're a high colonic
> You're the burning heat of a bridal suite in use
> You're the breasts of Venus
> You're King Kong's penis
> You're self-abuse!
> You're an arch in the Rome collection
> You're the starch in a groom's erection
> I'm a eunuch who has just been through an op
> But if Baby I'm the bottom
> You're the top!

> (The original, all seven verses—not including the above scatalogical parody—is from Porter's Anything Goes, 1934.)

The jeopardy in this, and all *objective* lyrics, is that the "YOU" (the listener) receives all the attention while the "I" (the singer) is no more interesting than the bearer of any message. In this example, the performer faces the further peril of having Mr. Porter's transcendent wit upstage the entire proceeding. Indeed, the singer could stand in the wings, unseen but not unheard, and gain the same audience reaction. To diminish the power of Cole Porter on the ear, one must magnify what meets the eye. We will *hear* about the "YOU"—she is admittedly " ... the top." What we need to *see* is her effect upon the singer (the "I"). *Objective lyrics require all the subjectivity the performer is able to invent.*

III.   The *Narrative* Lyric.

The giveaway: a story is being told in song.

> A fool sat beneath an olive tree
> And a wondrous thought had he
> So, he rose and he told it to the sky
> And where was I?

Behind the tree. I overheard his reverie.
"Why be content with an olive when you could have the tree?
Why be content to be nothing
When there's nothing you couldn't be?
Why be contented with one olive tree
When you could have the whole olive grove?
Why be content with a grove when you could have the world?"
The fool stood beneath the olive tree,
"What a wondrous thought!" said he.
"But, alas, it is very, very deep."
And then he yawned and went to sleep,
Because, you see, he was a fool.

("The Olive Tree," music and lyrics by Robert Wright and George Forrest, from *Kismet*, 1953. Copyright © 1953 Frank Music Corp. International copyright secured. All rights reserved. Used by permission.)

It is significant that as the categories of lyrics are defined, they become more jeopardizing. It is not that they should *not* be sung, only that their power to destroy the singer must be recognized from the start. The *narrative* lyric has much in common with the *subjective* song: the story may well turn out to be more interesting than the spinner of it. Narratives sung are no different than narratives spoken. They require one helluva storyteller. When the Caliph threatens to amputate the hands of Hajj the Beggar in *Kismet*, he sings "Gesticulate." As a professional whose livelihood depends on his skill in making a story quite literally pay off, he knows the importance of *seeing* a story told. By their very nature, *narrative* lyrics are better left to those who are able to *be* the narrator as well as *do* the narrative. The late Noel Coward, Danny Kaye, and the French chanteur Jacques Brel made something quite beautiful to behold when they performed this kind of high-style material, and today Charles Aznavour and Yves Montand (before he committed himself to acting) continue the French tradition. In general, I recommend this category be given wide berth unless it is evident from the start that the singer has chosen it for the very reason that he is able to do it.

IV. The *Instructive* Lyric.

I say to me every morning,
"You've only one life to live!
So why be done in? Let's let the sun in
And gloom can jump in the riv'.

No use to beat on the doldrums
Let's be imaginative
Each day is numbered
No good when slumbered
With only one life to live.
Why let the goblins upset you?
One smile and see how they run
And what does worrying net you?
Nothing! The thing is to have fun!
All this may sound kind of hackneyed
But it's the best I can give
Soon comes December,
So please remember
You've only one life to live.
Just one life to live!"

The *instructive* lyric is to be shunned almost as much as the narrative song. By definition, it is didactic and, like all sermons, belongs in the pulpit where those in attendance can either accept or reject the counsel. "How-to" dicta (even this volume) belong on bookshelves where one can read them or pass them by. It is no error that this kind of material is sung by eminently charming performers and given "production values" that mitigate the message. The beguiling "Put on a Happy Face," the self-righteous "Carefully Taught," the rhapsodic "Make Someone Happy," and the pseudoreligious "You'll Never Walk Alone" are all first-rate songs I cheerfully and willingly surrender to the next man. There are exceptions, of course, but I suggest the category be taken up tenderly. Perhaps they do not betray the amateur as much as the narrative lyric but, by their very statement, they tend not to beguile. The reader is forewarned.

V. The *Defiant* Lyric.

This category is self-explanatory. The title of the song tells it all: "Don't Rain on My Parade," "I'm the Greatest Star," "You're Gonna Hear from Me." If sing them you must, be sure you have been heard from already and with affection. It is not by accident that these songs are sung by the first plot line, namely, the star. I do not suggest them for audi-

11

tions but, since they purge anger and vent feelings, singing them can be cleansing—ideal material for the shower.

SHEET MUSIC

Just as the actor can buy the script of a play, the performer can purchase the script of a song: sheet music. It contains the lyric of the song, its melody, and the rhythm in which that melody is to be sung (see Chapter Two).

The lyric often, but not always, is composed of a Verse, followed by a Chorus. The latter may be referred to as the Refrain, and it is broken down into thematic divisions called 8s (again, see Chapter Two). Some random thoughts on the words you read on the sheet music you buy:

1. Unlike books and magazines, printed sheet music may be bowdlerised. Language has long been liberated, and smuggling salacious fiction through customs is now one of history's more quaint aberrations. Why sheet music remains purged of what can no longer be remotely considered offensive language is not certain. It is most likely traceable to the original purpose served by sheet music—songs to be played on the piano while the rest of the family, children as well as adults, stood around and sang along. Today it can be something of a shock to see "hell" printed as "h——," and maddening to read:

Couldn't sleep
And wouldn't sleep
When love came and told me I shouldn't sleep
Bewitched, bothered and bewildered am I.

when Lorenz Hart's original show lyric in *Pal Joey* was written to be sung:

Couldn't sleep
And wouldn't sleep
Until I could sleep where I shouldn't sleep
Bewitched, bothered and bewildered am I.

"God," thus named, is purged, as in the case of this Stephen Sondheim title-tune lyric. Its true version:

Do I hear a waltz?
Very odd, but I hear a waltz

12

There isn't a band
And I don't understand it at all.
I don't hear a waltz,
Oh my God! There it goes again!

In the printed sheet-music copy, the final line is replaced with " ... Oh my Lord! There it goes again!" which cuts the name of the deity with a fine-tooth comb at the same time that it destroys a very neat internal rhyme. "Gods," by virtue of its small 'g' is allowable: e.g. Porter's

The gods who nurse this universe
Think little of mortal's care, etc.

In recent years the unabridged collections of the lyrics of Cole Porter, Lorenz Hart, Oscar Hammerstein II, Ira Gershwin, and Stephen Sondheim's vocal scores and compact disc program notes have been published. If in possession of the writer's original words, should the performer correct these unfortunate launderings? Yes.

2. When shopping for a particular song, be prepared to be told by your local music-store proprietor that it is either no longer published or that it is available only in anthologies or in selections from the score that contains the desired number. If you elect to buy either, the cost not only rises but you will then own material for which you may have no use. Alternative sources can be found in libraries that boast music collections. In New York and Los Angeles—the two cities with which I am familiar—these can be treasure troves. Another suggestion: Copy the lyric from a recording of the song from its original show album and have a musical friend write out a lead sheet (the melodic line accompanied by basic chordal harmonies). This somewhat shady maneuver forbids you the professional use of the song without permission of the publisher but it does permit you to use it for purposes of acquiring work. No tampering or parodying of a lyric, whether a song is or is not published, is allowable without specific permission. In some cases the writer prohibits this practice under any circumstances.

3. Should you learn the Verse? Yes. If you are auditioning for a white-contract role (the contract signed by principals as distinguished from the pink contract intended for members of the chorus), you will seldom be asked to cut the Verse. The time allotted to each performer is more than sufficient to sing the entire song. However, remember that time is limited at a chorus call. In that instance, the writers and music director are primarily interested in your voice; the last "8" of a song that advertises your vocal range achieves its purpose by coming straight to the point.

   4.   The Verse is to the Chorus what exposition is to a play. It gives out *information* and furnishes the Chorus with its specificity. Remember: Songs from theater scores are written for a particular reason and are sung by a particular character in a particular situation at a particular time and place. If the dialogue (horizontal speech) that precedes the song is perceived as a steadily rising line toward the song's vocalization (vertical speech), the song, when it is extrapolated from its original context, is robbed of both its pertinence and its verticality. The Verse, then, aids in pushing the song up to the height it once enjoyed by virtue of its placement in the script. (For further explanation, see Chapter Seven, following Exercise Two: The Vamp.)

   However, exposition in a play or in a song (the Verse), albeit necessary, is a necessary evil. Information is not dramatic. It is worth considering singing the Verse in *ad lib* in order to *move* it. Ad lib is nothing more than the act of singing the melody of the lyric without its rhythmic scoring. When in doubt, *speak* the line and then sing it exactly as you have said it. Composers, aware of this possible choice, often make your task easier by consciously choosing to score the Verse as simply as possible. (Cole Porter's Verse for "Night and Day" is almost a monotone designed to imitate the "tick tick tock of the stately clock," which makes the arrival of the soaring line of the Chorus even more effective.) With practice one gains a certain facility with ad lib singing. You learn to *move* a line that has little interest or is a repeat of a line just sung and to slow down when something of importance is being said (sung). Speaking a line first to free it from its melody will lead you away from pouring out your heart on a, the, prepositions (for, from, in, at, etc.) and conjunctions (and, but, because, however) merely because they happen to fall on notes you love to hear yourself sing.

   5.   When you have sung a Verse in ad lib, the Chorus must be sung *in tempo* as scored. Unchecked ad lib suffers from the law of diminishing returns.

   6.   The lyric of the Chorus is the reason why you chose to sing the song. It is *your* script, invented by you at the instant we hear it sung and giving the illusion that it has never been sung before. This impression is maintained (as in acting) by proceeding from moment to moment and infusing those moments with an importance so great that you are, quite literally, impelled to sing what otherwise you might have chosen to speak.

   7.   Since a song well sung is one that appears to be your own and

is, therefore, your choice of language we will hear, look up any words or expressions in the lyric that you don't understand. Learn their meanings and their correct pronunciation.

ANALYSIS OF A LYRIC

The following lyric is written by Lorenz Hart:

VERSE A, B, C, D, E, F, G, I never learned to spell, at least not well.
1, 2, 3, 4, 5, 6, 7, I never learned to count a great amount.
But my busy mind is burning
To use what learning I've got
I won't waste any time
I'll strike while the iron is hot:
CHORUS If they ask me I could write a book
About the way you walk and whisper and look
I could write a preface on how we met
So the world would never forget
And the simple secret of the plot
Is just to tell them that I love you a lot
And the world discovers as my book ends
How to make two lovers of friends.

("I Could Write a Book," music and lyrics by Richard Rodgers and Lorenz Hart, from *Pal Joey*, 1940. Copyright © 1940 by Chappell and Co., Inc. Copyright renewed. International copyright secured. All rights reserved. Used by permission.)

All well-written ballad lyrics, once they are parted from their musical line, seem overlean. Remember: Lyrics are not poetry but light verse intended to be sung (see Chapter Three). Lorenz Hart was a master who invented love lyrics that, within the allowable margins permitted the show ballad, are consistently varied and cliché-free. "I Could Write a Book" is prime Hart: simple without being simplistic and held together with a schematic reference—in this case, the language that pertains to the writing of a book.

The Verse is pure exposition. Without it, the Chorus loses its special wit. A writer who writes a book is corroborating his choice of profession. In this instance, the man is not only not a writer, but undereducated, as well.

Because the Verse is expositional, we elect to sing it freely—in ad lib. I have said that when you *speak* a line, you will be more aware of

15

the weight of its language. Some lines will be sung *faster* because they are *less* interesting, while others will be delivered more *slowly* by virtue of their *importance*. How fast is fast and how slow is slow?

Speed, in show business, is not defined as it is on the Indianapolis Speedway or at the Kentucky Derby. At a race, speed implies *motion*—in the theater, it is *interest* that gives movement to the proceedings. All of us have endured watching a fast-paced farce that moves like a glacier through an endless evening, or sat through a play or a film that, though it "moves" slowly, keeps us enthralled.

In the case of "I Could Write a Book":

1. The first two lines should be delivered with some degree of speed since we can assume that our audience speaks English and counts numerals in their proper order as you do. If they had been written:

A ... F ... L ... T ... X ... B ... R ... Z, etc. and
1 ... 7 ... 3 ... 6 ... 9 ... 2 ... 8 ... 4, etc.

they would have been more interesting but that would have been another song. Remember: Your accompanist, whether a pianist or the conductor of an orchestra, speaks the same language you do; capricious ad lib line readings only make his job more troublesome.

2. The third line begins with the ubiquitous "But." If I were to list, in descending importance, the words lyricists call upon most often, they would arguably be: I, Me, You, Love, Free, Dream ... and But. In Verses, "but" would be nearer the top of the list, for when it appears you can be sure that what was being delivered as general information is now moving from first into second gear. It follows, then, that the speed of your ad lib reading will slow down with "but my busy mind is burning to use what learning I've got" because what you are about to say is more important to hear. Mr. Hart helps you by employing alliteration: " ... but my busy mind is burning ...," etc.

3. The fourth line: " ... I won't waste any time" should be read faster. The rule of thumb: A slow line (or possibly two) tends to be sandwiched between faster lines, and fast lines generally set up an important and therefore slower line reading.

4. The fifth and final line, "I'll strike while the iron is hot," owes its reading to yet another rule: In ad lib, when you have reached the line that precedes the end of ad lib—in this case, the first line of the Chorus—try to break up the line in as many places as possible without destroying sense. In telegram prose, then, the line will read something like this:

I won't waste any time (*stop*)
I'll strike (*stop*)
While the iron (*stop*) is hot:

These stops are not acting beats. They are Glottal Stops (see Chapter Three). Rendering the last line of the Verse in this manner permits the graceful transition from ad lib into "a tempo" singing without giving the impression that the Chorus has hit a stone wall.

5. We are now in the Chorus. "Tempo" ideally arrives on the downbeat of the last word of the Verse, in this case " ... hot." From there on, the song is sung as scored. The accompanist or conductor is king. The lyric will now be phrased according to the examples defined in Chapter Three.

Three cautionary rules:

1. " ... Walk and whisper and look": each verb should be clearly articulated or the line will sound like the name of a brokerage firm.

2. " ... Book ends": Be sure to put a glottal stop between the two words to distinguish them from brackets that hold up books. (See Chapter 17: "Bad English—Good Lyrics.")

3. If you elect to go out of tempo on the last line, "How to make two lovers ... of friends," remember: You may take whatever time you need when you are in ad lib, as long as you can make the silence meaningful. But the orchestra is waiting to rejoin you on the word " ... friends." To linger on " ... of" as in "How to make two lovers ... of .... friends" exposes you to a senseless reading (" ... of" is not a money word) and, worse, a sloppy downbeat on the Rideout that will begin on the last word " ... friends."

Words are the actor's stock in trade. Without them he is mute—no longer an actor but a mime. The words he *sings* are not to be considered less important than the clarity he bestows on them when he *speaks*. Lyrics can remain as dead as they are in print on the sheet music copy, or they can be given their life by virtue of the performer's ability to illuminate them. I do not want to downgrade the importance of good musical sound but, in the opera house, we tend to forgive what we see in direct ratio to what we hear: The more unique the voice of the *singer,* the more we forgive inept performing. That threshold of tolerance is considerably lower for the *actor-singer* who is a hyphenate for good reason: He straddles both the world of the theater and the world of song. Although it is not a prohibitive price placed on this duality, nevertheless it is one that must be paid.

17

2

Music: The Other Script

For the nonsinger who has just begun to sing, music can be an alien and intimidating language. There are new symbols to learn, styles of expressions, and even a special "grammar" with which one must gain fluency. It is not my purpose here to alarm the beginner by dwelling on musical theory and harmony, but if we agree that music—and, by extension, singing—is a language far different from the one we speak, nevertheless, unlike other foreign tongues, we hear and are subjected to music every day of our lives. And although we may not speak it well, all of us, to some degree, enjoy a fractional comprehension of it. No sophisticated musicianship, for example, is needed to identify a ballad, a lullaby, blues, a march, or a rock-and-roll vocal, and most of us can limp our way through a duet with whomever we hear on record or, as we move around a dance floor, softly sing into the ear of our partner. Standing still, we are all able to struggle through the anthem, jumping up and down octaves as the demands of the melody take precedence over nationalist fervor. At parties, "Happy Birthday"; on New Year's Eve, "Auld Lang Syne"; in church, beloved hymns—in all these instances we are able to raise our voices, unconcerned that our contribution to the total sonic effect may not measure up to professional standards. We can even give vent to our favorite songs and arias with full-out abandon, unchecked by any outside critical disdain, as long as we remain convinced that we are alone and unheard. None of this may strike the reader as particularly significant but it does make its point: The most abject beginner actor-singer is not as alien to the language of music as he may presume himself to be.

A point of interest: Just as the modality of the actor's performance in a play is decreed by the personal style of the playwright (one does not play Odets as one would interpret Sheridan or perform Simon in the manner of Shakespeare), a performance may be illuminated—at least in its early direction—by the distinctive signature of the composer and lyricist on their work. Just as Mozart is disparate from Tchaikovsky, so may a tune be recognized as Gershwin's rather than Cole Porter's. In each case, in the words of Alan Jay Lerner, the work "absolutely classifies him." Further: Gershwin, Rodgers and Hart (more than Rodgers and Hammerstein), Berlin, Porter, Frank Loesser, and Harold Arlen, among others, wrote songs that not only do not require sumptuous sound but may even be damaged when they are too "classically" vocalized. On the other hand, and still speaking generally, Leonard Bernstein's *Candide*, the more lavish Porter (e.g., "In the Still of the Night"), latter-day Burton Lane (*On a Clear Day You Can See Forever*), and Jerome Kern (*Showboat* and *The Cat and the Fiddle*)—again, among others—ask of their interpreters more, rather than less, opulent sound.

As for the work of the younger composers—Bock, Kander, Herman, Coleman, Webber, and Sondheim—the actor-singer can always find in their compositions material that he can perform well. However, the musical sophistication of these creative artists is always placed at the service of a musical's core statement. If the material is more "pop," as in the case of Sondheim's *Company*, for example, the less able singer will not be betrayed, whereas the demanding *Sweeney Todd* and *A Little Night Music* are not recommended to anyone who cannot meet the demands of the score. The same can be said of Andrew Lloyd Webber's *Evita* and *The Phantom of the Opera*, while his more accessible *Starlight Express* is well within the range of those whose voices are no more than they need be. In the case of that work, expert roller skating is of primary significance if frequency of cast replacements is an indication of order of importance. Discretion should always rule choice. As in the case of all second languages, singing instantly identifies the beginner, the resident alien, and the native-born.

CATEGORIES OF SONGS

Far fewer in number than those that define lyrics, the trade tends to divide songs into two loosely packaged groups.

I. The *Ballad*

An all-inclusive group: It can be a love song, blues, a folk song—whatever you would have it be—as long as it is *slow*. At an audition it serves a dual purpose:

a. for the composer, lyricist, and music director, it demonstrates the vocal competency of the auditionee;

b. for the librettist and the director, it presents the actor-singer as an interpreter of the text of the song.

As a teacher I can testify to the neophyte's queasy approach to a ballad. No amount of positive thinking can distract him away from an essential truth: A slow song cannot dissemble vocal inadequacy. No matter the excellence of his style of delivery of the lyric, this incontestable fact can be expected to work havoc with a performer's nervous system. The canny choice of song that plays up your way with a lyric while playing down your inability to sustain a purely vocal rendition can be seen to be a wise move but, in the final analysis, the more knowing members of the creative staff are those who are directly concerned with the score and its optimal presentation. They are hard to fool and must never be underestimated. The casting of a particular actor in a straight play depends on factors so subjective that one man's choice may very well be another's poison. Singing does not offer many hiding places. If they are wise, people sing what they can sing but, at the same time, listeners hear what they hear. There is only so much fancy footwork you can employ to upstage what your voice cannot quite cut.

II. The *Up-tempo* Song

As the ballad is defined by its slow tempo, the *Up-tempo* song is identified by the increased speed of its delivery. It is considerably less difficult to say of it that it is *not* slow than to remark that it is *fast*. How fast *is* fast? An *Up-tempo* song can be as slow-fast as a soft-shoe or a swing-waltz, as rapid-fire as Porter's "Blow, Gabriel, Blow," Gershwin's "I Got Rhythm," or Styne's "Everything's Coming Up Roses." Its lyric can be as easy and graceful as Hart's "Manhattan" or as complex as Gilbert's "I Am the Very Model of a Modern Major General." It can be as rousing as gospel and as godless as the raunchiest rock rouser. It is everything and anything *but it is never slow*. Unlike the *Ballad,* however, a stylish, swinging way with a lyric that "sings" can always move the attention of the listener away from a voice that, in the true definition of that word, cannot hold that attention.

SHEET MUSIC

Just as the printed lyric in the sheet-music copy of a song is not necessarily the lyricist's original version, so may the music be a simplification and even a truncation of its primary scoring. Verses and Interludes may be cut down or out; time signatures and note values altered to give the published copy a less intimidating appearance (evidence that the sheet music is intended for the novice pianist and not the vocalist); guitar cords added that belie not only the composer's intentions but worse, his knowledge of harmony. Unlike "serious" music, whose published scoring must be meticulously observed, the sheet music of a song does not, and indeed should not, demand rigid obedience. It is a reduced, even simplistic instrumental copy, and anything that will flesh out this flimsy skeleton is allowable. Short of outright alteration of the melody—and even this is no more than a venial sin—you are free to interpret the song in any manner you feel may be beneficial to its delivery. The term *arrangement* is nothing more than the personal signature of the arranger. It can be maintained that *whenever* you hear a song performed, you are, in fact, hearing an arrangement of the song.

In the previous chapter we broke down the printed lyric. Let us now examine the component musical parts to be found in the sheet-music copy of a song.

I. The *Vamp*

All printed copies of songs begin with a few bars of music called the *Vamp,* or *Intro.* It is recognizable as the first musical statement at the top of the copy and it is further identified by the absence of a lyric. How many bars make a Vamp? One, two, three, four, six, eight—but generally two to four bars are an adequate introduction. Sometimes the Vamp as printed is the creation of the composer who, not unreasonably, considers it an integral part of the whole, but it can be (and often is) a stale musical phrase of no creative significance invented by a nameless copyist in the employ of the publisher. In the case of the former, the songs of Sondheim and Arlen, for example, are true if somewhat simplified renderings of those composers' original scorings. However, at that moment when a song ceases to live on the page and, by its inevitable vocalization, is given its true life, the choice of Vamp—and its length—belongs to the performer. He may choose to retain the composer's introduction, or he and his arranger may elect a more personal and relevant musical statement.

One may do anything one chooses to do with a Vamp except live without it. It has three functions, only one of which must be considered essential.

1. The Vamp sets the key in which the song will be sung. Unless you are blessed with perfect pitch and can pick a note out of the air by thinking it, you will need to know the key you are going to be singing in and/or, by the end of the Vamp, your starting note. Does the audience need this information? No. But you do.

2. The Vamp establishes the tempo in which the song will be sung. No Vamp is designed to fool the audience. If a song is fast, the Vamp is equally and exactly that fast. If a song is slow, it will be just that slow. Is the tempo of the Vamp as important to you as your key or your starting note? No. You will know that you are going to sing "I Got Rhythm" and not "Memories," but it is good to hear how fast fast is. Does the audience care? Again, no. But again, there is an indeterminate advantage afforded the listener in hearing the rhythm of the language of the song before he is asked to attend the lyric and the melody.

3. Finally, the Vamp can function as your scene designer. By creative musical invention and within a minimum time span, the Vamp can paint an environment and color a musical/dramatic setting in which the performer's state of heart and mind will be given context. Do you always need this contribution? No. You can do without it, but there are songs that gain from an Intro that sets a mood as well as a key and a time signature. Does the audience need it? No, but, again, this richer Vamp can evoke an immediate emotional response to the country in which the still unheard song will live.

In the last forty years, within the performance of a musical, the *Bell Tone* has gained equal footing with the Vamp. It is the starting note, in all its nakedness, delivered by an instrument in the orchestra, that permits an exit out of dialogue into song with transitional grace and minimal expended time. In an audition, I strongly recommend the Vamp. You may not hear a Bell Tone when you nod to your pianist to begin to play, and there is nothing more pitiable than two Bell Tones when it is all too evident why the second one was required. However, if you are unwilling to surrender the declarative nature of a Bell Tone to a protracted Vamp, you can request a *Sting,* which is nothing more than a harmonized Bell Tone with a heavy stress on the top (your starting) note.

What determines the length of a Vamp from its shortest—the Bell Tone or the Sting—to its maximal number of bars? And what can be considered its optimal length? The answer lies both in the importance of the song's emotional climate and in the dramatic weight of the first line you will sing. A song that begins with "Once upon a time ... ," or "My name is ... ," or in the case of Rodgers and Hart's "I Could Write a Book": "A, B, C, D, E, F, G, etc." needs very little preparation of time. But were a song to begin with "Why was I born ... ?", or "Don't know why there's no sun up in the sky, stormy weather ... ," or "Southern trees bear a strange fruit, blood on the leaves and blood at the root ... ," more time is required. An ancillary consideration: The time it takes to say something as devastating as the opening lines of "Strange Fruit" will be the same whether or not you choose an accompanying Vamp. In fact, the preparation time can be just as effective with no music behind you *but* a Sting. There are silences that possess a shattering noise. In all cases, the choice of Vamp and its length will always be yours to make and substantiation for your choice will always be found in the song itself.

Every Vamp possesses an inevitability factor: its implicit death. It is inevitable that a Vamp will die at that exact moment when the first word of the song is born. That word may be the first word of the Verse or, if there is none, the first word of the Chorus.

II. The *Verse*

The Verse follows the Vamp and is the first vocalizing of the text of the song. As noted above, the Verse seldom contains heavyweight musical material. Since it is so scored in order to give preeminence to the information contained in the lyric, most often Verses can be ad libbed without effort; e.g., in "I Could Write a Book," the first eight bars are sung on almost one note. Rodgers's genius for setting words to music is evident as he increases the melodic invention on the third line when the lyric starts its ascent out of the general into the specific, moving with ever-increasing musical tension toward the final line of the Verse.

The generalization that all Verses surrender their musical eminence to the priority of the lyric has many exceptions. Composers are as idiosyncratic as playwrights. Vernon Duke, who wrote symphonic and chamber music under the name of Vladimir Dukelsky (it was Gershwin who suggested the Americanized name that appeared on all his music after 1955), wrote Verses to his theater songs that are so complicated they must be studied to be learned. The Choruses that follow these mini-études are downright simplistic. Gershwin, too, wrote Verses that are often as interesting, if not commercially apparent, as his Choruses (e.g., the Verses to "I Can't Be Bothered Now," "Nice Work If You Can Get It," "Beginner's Luck," "Slap That Bass," "A Foggy Day," and "Let's

Kiss and Make Up"), but rarely does a first-rate song possess a Verse more satisfying than its Chorus. (The Chorus of Gershwin's "The Man I Love" was originally the Verse to a nameless song no one has ever heard. Ira Gershwin, in his *Lyrics on Several Occasions* [New York: Viking, 1959], reports that the melody was too heavyweight as a Verse. Somewhat modified and with a new Verse of its own, it was added to the score of *Lady Be Good*, this time as a Chorus. The inversion must have been a sound one for, as a Chorus, it became a major standard in the Gershwin folio.)

III. The *Chorus*

The Chorus is the song. Its melody is all. At the turn of the century, and continuing well into the sixties, Choruses were composed and shaped within thirty-two bars of music. It is astonishing how much variety was achieved within so tight a formula consisting, as it did, of only four eight-bar musical phrases—sensibly called "8s."

Each "8" is given a letter name—the first "8" is always referred to by the letter "A." (The rigidity of the thirty-two-bar Chorus long ago yielded to looser song forms in which "8s" may be composed of themes as long as ten, twelve, or more bars but, whatever their length, the term "8" is still used as a label for each musical theme.)

1. AABA. If the first "8" is identified by the letter "A" and the next eight-bar phrase is repeated (often identically), the second "8" is also referred to as "A." The third "8," always called the Bridge or the Release and always consisting of new thematic material, is designated by the letter "B." The fourth "8," referred to as the *Last 8,* recalls the first theme—with a possible variation—and is again labeled "A." The thirty-two-bar song form, AABA, can still be heard in the land. Among the great AABA standards: "The Man I Love," "Some Enchanted Evening," "Where or When," "I Get a Kick Out of You," "Smoke Gets in Your Eyes," "Send in the Clowns," "Hello, Dolly!," "New York, New York" and ... and ...

2. ABAB. When the second "8" is a different musical theme, it is referred to by the letter "B." The third "8," a reprise of the first "8," recalls the letter-name "A" and the last "8," completing the thirty-two bars, repeats (again, with a possible variation) the second theme and its designated name is therefore "B." This song form, ABAB, is also found in countless standards: "I Got Lost in His Arms," "A Foggy Day," "Time After Time," "Embraceable You," "People," "Falling in Love with Love," and our model song, "I Could Write a Book."

3. There are variations on the classic AABA and ABAB song forms.

Just as the bar count of any "8" may contain more than eight bars of music, so may more complicated thematic material be found in a Chorus. For example: ABCA, ABAC, etc. But theater music, like its counterparts (country-western, middle-of-the-road, and even rock and roll), does not stray too far from themes that are not only easy to hear but are easily memorable because of thematic repetition.

(Although Sondheim composes within the established rigid song forms listed above, e.g., "Anyone Can Whistle" [ABAB] and "Send in the Clowns" [AABA], his recent work stresses minimal recapitulation within the body of each song. Instead, thematic reprises of motifs relevant to character are woven into the musical matrix of the entire work, as in *Sunday in the Park With George* and *Into the Woods*. As a consequence, the performer finds fewer songs that can be lifted out of their context without suffering a loss of power and general comprehensibility. The more formalist writing in *Sweeney Todd* ["Not While I'm Around," ABAB] and "No One Is Alone" from *Into the Woods* [AABA], in combination with their less parochial lyrics, gives these songs a distinctive emotional singularity that, in part, is due to a subtle recognition of their neoromantic structure.)

IV. The *Rideout*

The Rideout is the music that begins on the downbeat of the last word of the song. Just as all songs have a Vamp, every Chorus comes packaged with a Rideout. The actor has no problem with a Vamp: He understands the need for "preparation." But a Rideout exists only in the world of sung speech. One *says,* "I love you" period, but one *sings* "I love youuuuuuuu," period. The Rideout is the music that continues under and through that held last word and, while the Vamp affords an ascent *into* the song, a Rideout furnishes the singer with the descent *out* of the world of sung language.

Like the Vamp, Rideouts come in all lengths. They can be as short as a simple Sting (one chord, like the blast of a trumpet) or be stretched into a Roxy Rideout, putatively named after the last Roxyette (grandmother of today's Rockettes, who still work the stage of Radio City Music Hall in New York City) had kicked her way into the wings.

The Rideout, as printed in the sheet music of a song, is usually two to four bars long but, again, it can be as long as you choose to make it. One caution: The Roxy Rideout was designed to elicit a Pavlovian response from an audience. They hear its call and, like dogs who salivate in response to the sound of a bell, they applaud. In a musical, a song that might have elicited no response at all can gain an ovation by the mere expedient of the addition of a Roxy Rideout. At an audition, this reaction is denied you. There is no one present to applaud save those who are auditioning you. Since they are not there to be entertained but to cast the show, a good audition tends to create a silence in which whispered confidences are held and decisions are made. Unless you are able to turn on an applause machine in your head that will cover the appalling silence, I would shun a lengthy Rideout. Remember: The Rideout's sole contribution is to get you out of the song and back into the real world. Your descent will be judged by how gracefully you execute it.

V. *Air*

The Vamp, the Verse if there is one, and the Chorus (composed of "8s"), ending with the Rideout, constitute the component parts of the printed sheet-music copy. But there is music that exists between the sung lines—"fills"—that can be described as the "Air" in the song. If "Air" is recognized as *music without words,* the Vamp and Rideout, too, must be listed as "Air" pockets. All songs, both serious and popular (in the classic meaning of these words), possess "Air." But all "Air" is not of equal significance.

In order of importance:

1. The Vamp holds first position since it heralds the arrival of the song and because it is the most difficult to perform with style. Nothing betrays the amateur more than his inability to leave the world of reality and make the singing of what he has to say seem to have been inevitable.

2. The Rideout—for the reverse reason.

3. If there is a Verse, the "Air" that follows its end and precedes the arrival of the Chorus.

4. If the song is AABA, the "Air" that *precedes* the arrival of the Bridge, or Release (the third "8").

5. The "Air" between the end of the Bridge, or Release, and the last "8."

6. The last remaining pocket: the "Air" between the first and the second "8."

With the addition of "Air," the musical shape of the sheet music copy of our model song now reads in this somewhat absurd fashion:

VAMP   (*Air*)
VERSE   A, B, C, D, E, F, G, H, I never learned to spell
At least, not well. (*Air*)

	1, 2, 3, 4, 5, 6, 7, I never learned to count
	A great amount. (*Air*)
	But my busy mind is burning
	To use what learning I've got (*Air*)
	I won't waste any time (*Air*)
	I'll strike (*Air*)
	While the iron (*Air*)
	Is hot (*Air*)
CHORUS	If they asked me I could write a book
1ST "8" (A)	About the way you walk and whisper and look (*Air*)
2ND "8" (B)	I could write a preface on how we met
	So the world would never forget (*Air*)
3RD "8" (A)	And the simple secret of the plot
	Is just to tell them that I love you a lot (*Air*)
LAST "8" (B)	And the world discovers as my book ends
	How to make two lovers (*Air*)
	Of friends (*Air*)
RIDEOUT	(*Air*)

These musical pockets of "Air" are integral. They give mathematical shape to the sung phrase and are to be considered as much a part of the song as the melody and the words. The lack of an accompanying lyric in no way diminishes their importance. "Air" comes in all lengths, from the simple Bell Tone (e.g., the "Air" in the above Verse after " ... I won't waste any time," after " ... I'll strike," and after " ... While the iron") to long and difficult-to-sustain "fills." When the performer inherits "Air" that seems to him unnecessarily overlong, I have always found that the composer is considerably brighter than first hearing may have indicated. Since "Air" cannot be arbitrarily cut, the singer is faced with no alternative but to deal with it. Second hearing confirms how psychologically sound even the longest "Air" pocket may be. (There are rare cases in which protracted musical phrases without lyric—"Air"—are found in the published sheet music [as set apart from the vocal score of the musical]. This may be due to the composer's demand to retain the "Air" and, as such, must be executed as printed. However, I have seen songs in which "Air," retained from the vocal score, is just plain over-long. In the production, it served to cover important physical and/or staging activity. In these cases I am impelled to shorten or even cut the "Air" when it is evident that, in an audition of the song, it would be impossible to fill. However, remember that cuts are surgeries and they are not to be performed lightly.)

VI. *Rhythm*

Music is binary. It consists of a melody wedded to a rhythmic pulse. Until now, we have spoken only of melodies (and the words assigned to them), but they share, in equal importance, the rhythms in which they are scored. Instructions concerning those rhythms are indicated at the top of the sheet music copy, immediately following the identification of the song's key signature. It appears as a numerical fraction that decrees the number of beat impulses in each bar of music and the note value that equals one of those beats. For example, the time signature 2/4 informs you that there are two beats in each bar of music (the 2 of the fraction) and that each beat is equal to a quarter-note (1/4) or its equivalent (two eighth notes, four sixteenth notes, etc. Ergo 2 x 1/4 = 2/4). In contrast to the bottomless pit from which an infinity of melodies can be created, there is a limited number of rhythms in which those melodies come packaged.

1. *2/4 time signature* (see explanation above). The first beat of a bar of music is called the *downbeat* and the beat that precedes it is the *upbeat*. Since there are only two beats in a bar of 2/4 time, each bar contains both a downbeat and an upbeat. If you were to underline the downbeat and leave the upbeat unmarked, it would read 1, 2/1, 2/1, 2/, etc. There is about the 2/4 time signature a redolence reminiscent of a show business that is long gone but one that excites audiences who, all too willingly, slip back into the excitement it recalls. When Rose sings "Everything's Coming Up Roses" in the first-act finale of Jule Styne and Stephen Sondheim's *Gypsy,* she sings it in "cut time" (a pulse that has two beats in each bar), thereby manipulating the reaction of the audience with astonishing power. Cole Porter's cut-time "Just One of Those Things" and the Gershwins' "Love Is Sweeping the Country," in 2/4 time, have the same joyous, if somewhat old-fashioned, tone that evokes a more innocent time. This rhythm is seldom employed today unless the script requires it.

2. *3/4 time-signature.* Here there are three beats in each measure or bar, with each beat equal to a quarter-note or its equivalent. In the following example, the downbeat and the upbeat are underlined: 1, 2, 3/1, 2, 3/1, 2, 3/, etc. This time signature, one that the world recognizes as a waltz, is not always a bit of transplanted Vienna. There is the slow, stately waltz called *valse triste,* in which the Viennese oom-pah-pah, oom-pah-pah is replaced by a bar of music that contains three equally stressed beats. "Melinda" by Burton Lane and Alan Jay Lerner from their score for *On a Clear Day You Can See Forever,* "Days Gone By" from Bock and Harnick's *She Loves Me,* and "I Still See Elisa" from Lerner and

29

Loewe's *Paint Your Wagon* are, all three, lovely examples of this song form. An American stamp is placed on the swing or jazz waltz that gives its 3/4 time signature an irresistible gaiety. Listen to the standard "I'm All Smiles" from Michael Leonard and Herbert Martin's score for *The Yearling* and Elmer Bernstein and Carolyn Leigh's "Walk Away" from *How Now Dow Jones*.

3. *4/4 time signature.* Here there are four beats in each measure or bar, with each beat equal to a quarter-note or its equivalent. Underlining both the downbeat and the upbeat, it would read: 1, 2, 3, 4/1, 2, 3, 4/1, 2, 3, 4, etc.

This 4/4 time is by far the most common time signature. Blues, ballads, gospel, country-western, rock and roll, disco, tangos, rhumbas, sambas, bossa novas, congas—almost every song we hear on our radios, background movie scores to the films we go to see or rent to view, cassettes, MTVs, CDs, and reel-to-reels—when all this music that fills our lives is not a waltz, it is probably coming to us in the 4/4 time signature.

4. *5/4 time signature.* This is rare in theater music, and though it would be described thus—1, 2, 3, 4, 5/1, 2, 3, 4, 5/, etc., it is far easier to conduct and/or to think of it as a combination of 3/4 time plus 2/4 time: 1, 2, 3/1, 2/1, 2, 3/1, 2/, etc. The song "Sensitivity" from *Once Upon a Mattress* owes much of its wit, apart from the lyric, to the 5/4 time signature.

5. *6/8 time signature.* Each measure or bar has six beats and each beat is an eighth-note or its equivalent. This rhythm is conducted, like 2/4 time, with only a downbeat and an upbeat defining the bar, but each gesture indicates *three* beats: 1, 2, 3, 4, 5, 6/1, 2, 3, 4, 5, 6/, etc. The time signature has a rousing effect on an audience. Marches, most often scored in 4/4 time, can be composed in 6/8 time without any loss of excitement, e.g., Meredith Willson's "Seventy-six Trombones" from *The Music Man,* "Buckle Down Winsockie" from Martin and Blane's *Best Foot Forward,* and Styne and Sondheim's "Mr. Goldstone" from their score for *Gypsy.* Jigs are also written in this time signature, e.g., "My Mother's Wedding Day" from Lerner and Loewe's Scottish *Brigadoon.*

And that is about the sum total of the rhythms you will meet. There are additional time signatures (6/4, 9/4, and even 12/4), but they are only extended versions of 3/4 time. Stephen Sondheim's entire scoring of *A Little Night Music* is in waltz time and its variations. Within the composer's predetermination to keep each element of the score rooted in the Viennese ambience of the script (although its seminal life was Ingmar Bergman's Swedish film *Smiles of a Summer Night*), the extraordinary variety he was able to create out of this limited palette of rhythmic patterns is awesome. There is not a whisper of 3/4 time to be heard in "Send in the Clowns" and yet it is written in multiples of that very time-signature.

In conclusion: Sheet music, as stated above, is a scored version of a song simplified down from the composer's original—and more complex harmonic plan—in order to enable the beginner to play the song without difficulty. A song can even be sung without accompaniment, and when it is absent it is said to be sung *a cappella* (in chapel style). It is best kept in a chapel and not at an audition.

3

Phrasing

A world of thought in one translucent phrase.
                                              —Henry Bernard Carpenter

PHRASING FROM LYRIC

What language *says* is made clear to an audience to the degree that the actor articulates and projects it audibly. What words *mean* is given clarity only when the speaker comprehends them, and this comprehension is manifest only when his language is well phrased.

The addition of music to text offers the actor-singer two choices: 1) He can phrase a song by using its lyric as a point of departure; or, 2) He may choose to phrase from the music, using *its* demands to determine his primary choices. I begin with phrasing from lyric on the assumption that the performer finds his natural home in the words, rather than the music, of a song.

To begin with, write the lyric down in your own handwriting. Only then will you be able to see it as script, isolated from its musical setting. In the previous chapter, I mentioned the need to take up the naked lyric tenderly. Remember: It is not poetry and, deprived of music, it may seem trivial. (In his preface to *Lyrics on Several Occasions* [New York:

Viking, 1959, p. xi], Ira Gershwin says: "Lyrics are arrived at by fitting words mosaically to music. Any resemblance to actual poetry, living or dead, is highly improbable.") However, the work of Ogden Nash, Cole Porter, Ira Gershwin, Lorenz Hart, Yip Harburg, Johnny Mercer, and Stephen Sondheim can read much like, and even pass for, light verse. By way of example, this Verse written by Nash:

> When you look life in the face
> There's too much time
> There's too much space
> There's too much future, too much past
> Man is so little and the world so vast.
> You may fancy yourself as an immortal creature
> But you're just the cartoon between ...
>   A double-feature.

> ("Roundabout," music and lyrics by Vernon Duke and Ogden Nash, from *Two's Company,* 1952. Copyright 1946, Warner Bros., Inc. Copyright renewed. All rights reserved. Used by permission.)

or, from the pen of Cole Porter, the Verse of "Red, Hot and Blue":

> Due to the tragic lowness of my brow
> All music that's highbrow gets me upset.
> I don't like Schubert's music or Schumann's
> I'm one of those humans who only goes in
> For Berlin, or Vincent Youmans.

> (Music and lyrics by Cole Porter, from the show of the same name, 1936. Copyright © 1936 by Chappell & Co., Inc. Copyright renewed. International copyright secured. All rights reserved. Used by permission.)

I have chosen as a model lyric, and as a model lyric for phrasing from lyric, Lorenz Hart's "The Most Beautiful Girl in the World":

> 1ST "8" The most beautiful girl in the world
>   (A) Picks my ties out
>   Eats my candy
>   Drinks my brandy
>   The most beautiful girl in the world
> 2ND "8" The most beautiful star in the world
>   (A) Isn't Garbo
>   Isn't Dietrich

But that sweet trick
Who can make me believe it's a beautiful world
BRIDGE OR   Social? Not a bit
RELEASE   Nat'ral kind of wit
(B)   She'd shine anywhere
And she hasn't got platinum hair.
LAST "8"   The most beautiful house in the world
(A)   Has a mortgage
What do I care?
It's goodbye care
When my slippers are next
To the ones that belong
To the one and only
Beautiful girl in the world.

("The Most Beautiful Girl in the World," music and lyrics by Richard Rodgers and Lorenz Hart, from *Jumbo*, 1935. Copyright © 1935 T. B. Harms Company. Copyright Renewed. All rights reserved, including the right of public performance for profit. International copyright secured. Made in the U.S.A. by permission.)

Qualitative values are more readily appreciated when the words are separated from what, in this case, is a ravishing waltz.

1. There is wit at work here.

2. Hart's affection for Savoy rhyming is evident, for example, in "Dietrich ... sweet trick." (The works of Gilbert and Sullivan were staged at London's Savoy Theater. It gave its name to aficionados—Savoyards—of Gilbert's unique gift for rhyming.)

3. AABA in form, the lengthy title in the first line of the first "8" is set off by three short lines and repeated for the sake of balance and the shape of things. The title is never stated in quite the same way again.

4. The lengthening of the title at the end of the second "8" promotes a swelling that will be corroborated by the music.

5. The Bridge could not be tighter and, in the negative, tells us a great deal about what the "most beautiful girl" is not.

6. The last "8" further lengthens the title by adding a reaffirmation of her superlative singularity.

Further study of the lyric furnishes more information. Lyric category: Objective. It will need *subjectivizing* to make it work. Mr. Hart helps out with a liberal sprinkling of editorial comments that betray the personal taste of the performer of the song. For example:

1. "Picks my ties out"—a minor revelation but nevertheless most men prefer to pick out their own ties. Women know this so well that, as they hand a man a gift box containing a tie, they say, as a matter of course, "If you don't like it, they will exchange it." The lady in this lyric and the man extolling her share a similar taste in ties.

2. "Drinks my brandy"—a postprandial drink that implies intimacy.

3. "Who can make me believe it's a beautiful world"—sheer irony when one considers the daily newspapers and late-night news programs.

4. "Social? Not a bit"—we know what the gentleman thinks of those who are …

5. "Nat'ral kind of wit"—of those who manufacture it …

6. "And she hasn't got platinum hair"—of those who have it.

Plot One

In its first plotting, we are impelled to make sense out of language by linking words and phrases together within one arc of breath, from its inspiration to its expiration. Breathing is an involuntary act, but one can voluntarily husband it or waste it. Using a checkmark to represent the intake of breath, and with only grammar to justify it, *Plot One's* sole purpose is to separate one subject and its predicate from the next subject and predicate. Of course, a breath (✓) precedes the first line.

> The most beautiful girl in the world
> Picks my ties out (✓)
> Eats my candy (✓) (*The title line of the song is implied.*)
> Drinks my brandy (✓) (*Again, the title is implied.*)
> The most beautiful girl in the world (✓)
> The most beautiful star in the world
> Isn't Garbo (✓)
> Isn't Dietrich (✓) (*The first line of the 2nd "8" is implied.*)
> But that sweet trick
> Who can make me believe it's a beautiful world (✓)
> Social? (✓) (*"Is she" is implied.*) Not a bit (✓)
> Nat'ral kind of wit (✓) (*"She has a" is implied.*)
> She'd shine anywhere
> And she hasn't got platinum hair (✓)
> The most beautiful house in the world
> Has a mortgage (✓)
> What do I care? (✓)
> It's goodbye care

When my slippers are next
To the ones that belong
To the one and only
Beautiful girl in the world (✓)

After you have worked out the preceding plot, call in the pianist and sing through what you have marked, taking a breath wherever you have indicated one. It will be apparent that, in some places, you will not need a breath and in others you will have so much breath that further inspiration is impossible. These conclusions are not absolutes, depending as they do on your ability to take, sustain, and utilize the breath you take, but within these margins, it will be clear that *Plot Two* is in order. For example:

" ... Eats my candy" *You will not need a breath here. Deprived of it, you will be able to proceed comfortably.*

" ... Isn't Dietrich" (✓) *The same may be true here. But a longer line follows it and discretion should be the rule. More of that later.*

" ... Social" (✓) *This breath is impossible since you have just filled up at the end of the preceding line.*

" ... Has a mortgage" (✓) *As with " ... Eats my candy," not needed.*

" ... It's goodbye care" *True, we have been faithful to the rule of "one subject and predicate = one breath" rule, but here it is almost impossible to sing this sentence, followed by the Rideout, at the top of your range. And even if you can, it is unnecessary self-advertising. The rule, then: breathe where the least damage is done to the text. More often than not, this will be before articles, conjunctions, and/or prepositions.*

"When my slippers are next" (✓)
"To the ones that belong" (✓)
"To the one and only beautiful girl" (✓)
"In the world" (✓). *You need not take all three breaths. The second of the three is apt to be the most valuable, but the third breath is a distinct possibility in view of the impending vocal demands of the Rideout.*

Plot Two

Plot Two takes Plot One into consideration. But remember: The impulse that dictates the breaths we marked is still operative. In place of the "cut" breaths we will insert a Glottal Stop or Glottal Catch (a "comma" in the vocal line that interrupts the column of air as it passes through the larynx) in order to retain the separation of subjects and predicates.

There is a further value the Glottal Stop offers: When you have a particular word in your lyric that needs "highlighting," the placement of a Glottal Stop immediately before the word will give it prominence within the body of the line. For example, a Glottal Stop in the Bridge between " ... shine" and " ... anywhere." " ... She'd shine anywhere" is far less a compliment than " ... she'd shine (,) anywhere." Again, a Glottal Stop between " ... got" and " ... platinum hair" would underline the gentleman's dislike of platinum hair. Lastly, on paper, " ... What do I care? It's goodbye care ... etc." makes sense. We understand that the first " ... care" is a verb and the second is a noun, as in woe or trouble. When the line is sung, however, the rhyme " ... *I* care" and " ... *goodbye* care" is all we hear. A Glottal Stop between " ... goodbye (,) care" restores the sense of the line without damaging Mr. Rodgers's melody. When you speak the lines in this paragraph aloud you will understand more clearly the value of the contribution made by the insertion of the Glottal Stops.

> The most beautiful girl in the world
> Picks my ties out (,)
> Eats my candy (,)
> Drinks my brandy (✓)
> The most beautiful girl in the world (✓)
> The most beautiful star in the world
> Isn't Garbo (,)
> Isn't Dietrich (✓)
> But that sweet trick
> Who can make me believe it's a beautiful world (✓)
> Social (,) not a <u>bit</u> (✓)
> Nat'ral kind of <u>wit</u> (✓)
> She'd shine (,) anywhere
> And she hasn't got (,) platinum hair (✓)
> The most beautiful house in the world
> Has a mortgage (,)
> What do I care? (✓)

It's goodbye (,) care
When my slippers are next (✓)?
To the ones that belong (✓)
To the one and only beautiful girl (✓)
In the world (✓)

If Plot Two is comfortable for you, freeze it. If not, go on to a third plotting. Remember: What you can do with ease in the privacy of your home may desert you in the less congenial atmosphere of an audition or a performance. When there is a question, give yourself both the benefit of the doubt and more breath marks. When confidence goes, so will your breath.

When you have settled on the final phrasing plotting, enter all breath marks, Glottal Stops, and pertinent information on your sheet music copy. It will be your personal script, recallable whenever you pick up the song. In the case of our model lyric, pertinent information would include:

1. In the Bridge, the line " ... Social, not a bit" is scored to be held for two bars, but doing so destroys the onomatopoeic value of the word " ... bit." Underline it as indicated so that you remember to get off the word and thereby reinforce the gentleman's distaste for social pretension.

2. The word " ... wit," in the next line, is not a word that sounds like what it means, but it is not aided by being held. There is no musical gold to be found in the vowel sound "ih." Double-underline it, again as indicated, to remember *not* to pay attention to the rhythmic scoring of the word.

Finally, two exceptions to these ground rules for phrasing from lyric.

1. Most important of all: When you need a breath, take one! Do not sacrifice your life on the altar of a phrasing plotting. The audience will not understand the suicide. In fact, phrasing can be defined as good when those who listen to you are unaware of how you achieve your results. Remember: Breathe with your lungs and not your mind. Any breath can be camouflaged behind the cover of an inspired bit of acting.

2. Although a Rideout is alien to the actor, the performer meets up with it at the finish of everything he sings. At its most extended—the Roxy Rideout—it may even be the major factor that triggers the audience's affectionate response. Not only does a Rideout tend to protract, but because it does so at the peak of your vocal range, you will need breath to support it. On paper, when phrasing from lyric would argue against the idea of grabbing a breath immediately before the last word

> When my slippers are next
> To the ones that belong (✓)
> To the one and only
> Beautiful girl in the (✓) world

it is not in the least appalling when the line is sung. You will be able to sustain the Rideout with no loss of energy, secure in the knowledge that you have the breath to spin it out.

PHRASING FROM MUSIC

Songs are sung scripts. Phrasing from lyric introduces the actor-singer to the subject by allowing him, in the beginning, to live in a country in which he is still at home: words. But words that you sing are expressed in a far more emotional and universal language—music—a language that has its own rules and its own figures of sung speech. We move on to the more difficult subject of phrasing from music.

Choices now need not be governed by good grammar but will stem from what the singer "hears." As a recommended course of study, listen to the recordings of Frank Sinatra, Mel Tormé, Cleo Laine, and Peggy Lee. They are *musical* vocalists whose voices—along with their understanding of the words—are put to the service of the songs they sing. Exposure to excellence cannot help but refine your understanding of their art.

Among the many possibilities that phrasing from music offers you:

I. Enharmonic Changes

Simply stated, modulation permits a song to leave the home key in which it is scored. Rules define how the composer may do it but he is free to move through key changes as long as he obeys the rules of modulation. To understand an enharmonic change, imagine a piano keyboard. Each key does double and sometimes triple duty: C Sharp may be read as D Flat, D Sharp as E Flat, F as E Sharp, F Sharp as G Flat as well as E Double-Sharp, G Sharp as A Flat, etc. The pitch stays the same; only the name of the note changes. It can be seen that renaming a note places it in the context of a new key. For example: If we think of G Sharp as the third, or the *mi,* of the key of E Major, by the simple act of name-changing G Sharp to A Flat, it becomes the *do* of the key of A Flat. The change is called *enharmonic* and when it occurs, the rules of modulation are put aside.

When an enharmonic change appears in the *vocal line,* it is bad taste musically to breathe as the change is going on. Even if you must take a breath before or after the enharmonic change—a breath that, on paper, makes no sense at all—the positive value of the musical phrasing will be its own justification. For example, Oscar Hammerstein's lyric to the Bridge and the first line of the last "8" of Jerome Kern's "All the Things You Are," *phrased from lyric,* would read:

You are the angel glow
That lights a star (✓)
The dearest things I know
Are what you are (✓)
Someday my happy arms will hold you, etc.

However, there is an enharmonic change on the last word of the Bridge, " … are." Kern has scored the song in the key of A Flat (a key for four flats in its signature), but, using time-honored rules of modulation, the Bridge finds itself in the key of E Major (with four sharps in its signature). The word " … are" falls on a G Sharp (the third or *mi* of the key of E Major). By coincidence (again, check your piano), G Sharp is also A Flat and so, with an enharmonic change available to the composer, the "Some … " of "Someday" finds us back where we began at the top of the Chorus—in the original key of A Flat—with this simple and, when sung, exquisite enharmonic modulation. To breathe while the change is going on would be destructive of Kern's intention. Phrasing from lyric yields to the demands of the music: the singer can be said to have joined the boys in the band. The new phrasing chart should now read:

You are the angel glow
That lights a star (✓)
The dearest things I know (✓)
Are what you are ⌒
⌣ Someday my happy arms will hold you … (✓), etc.

("All the Things You Are" by Jerome Kern and Oscar Hammerstein II, from *Very Warm for May,* 1939. Copyright © 1939 T. B. Harms Company. Copyright renewed. All rights reserved including the right of public performance for profit. International copyright secured. Made in U.S.A. Used by permission.)

41

By taking a breath in the wrong place (lyrically speaking) after " ... know" (at the end of the third line of the Bridge), you will have enough breath to slide the last word of the Bridge, " ... are," to the next line, beginning with " ... Someday." If you cannot make it all the way through to " ... hold you," grab for a breath after " ... Someday" when the coast is clear.

A second example, again by Jerome Kern:

> Long ago and far away
> I dreamed a dream one day
> and now that dream is here beside me
> Long the skies were overcast ... etc.

> ("Long Ago and Far Away," music and lyrics by Jerome Kern and Ira Gershwin, from the film *Cover Girl,* 1944. Copyright © 1944 by T. B. Harms Company. Copyright renewed. All rights reserved including right of performance for profit. International copyright secured. Made in U.S.A. Used by permission.)

Phrased from lyric, a correct plotting would be:

> Long ago and far away
> I dreamed a dream one day (✓)
> And now that dream is here beside me (✓)
> Long the skies were overcast ... etc.

But Kern has scored an enharmonic change on " ... beside me" that rides over the bar into " ... Long the skies were overcast." To give it its due, phrasing from the music would change the plotting to:

> Long ago and far away (✓)
> I dreamed a dream one day
> And now (✓) that dream is here beside me ⌒
> ⌣Long the skies were overcast (✓) ... etc.

By placing breath marks where they will service the *musical* demands of a song rather than the *lyrical* sense of its script, awkward choices on paper become graceful musical statements when they are sung. In the case of enharmonic changes, there is no choice of direction between phrasing from lyric and phrasing from music: *Music should always take precedence.*

II. Over-the-Bar

Phrasing from music becomes more difficult when the reader is not able to hear its "sound." However, another procedure—over-the-bar phrasing—can be described. This arbitrary device is achieved by the singer's choosing not to breathe until the lyric phrase has passed "over-the-bar" line, whether or not the sense of the text is served. The following lyric, by Johnny Mercer, to the music of Harold Arlen, first phrased from lyric:

I promise you a faithful heart (✓)
One that has always been free (✓)
At night there's a handful of stars
That I pretend belong to me (✓)
I promise you (✓) that rich or poor
    (The breath after "I promise you" prepares for the high note on the
    word "poor." See lead sheet on page 46.)
I would be happy to share
The arms you have taken possession of (✓)
The sun in the meadow (✓)
The fire in the shadows (✓)
And I promise you I'll be there (✓)

("I Promise You," music and lyrics by Harold Arlen and Johnny Mercer, from the film *Here Come the Waves,* 1944. Copyright © 1944 by Harwin Music Corp. Copyright renewed. Used by permission.)

Disregarding the inherent sense of the above plotting, over-the-bar phrasing would read:

I promise you a faithful heart
One (✓) that has always been free
At night (✓) there's a handful of stars
That I pretend belong to me (✓)
I promise you (✓) that rich or poor
I would be happy to share
The arms (✓) you have taken possession of
The sun (✓) in the meadow
The fire (✓) in the shadows
And I promise you I'll be there (✓)

No sensible reason motivates this phrasing, but when you hear it sung, its musical validity is evident. Over-the-bar provides a dramatic and emotional thrust that does not allow the listener to relax when the "Air" fill arrives at the end of the line. I have used this song as an example only because it offers more than one opportunity to phrase over-the-bar. Not all songs are this accommodating. Most often, you will phrase with whatever tools you need—either from lyric or from music—to gain maximum illumination of the text and the melody of what you sing.

That country called "Jeopardy," which Mr. Lardner claimed is the minefield all of show business lives over and in, is made less hazardous with each element you add to a song that will help it gain and hold the attention of the listener. Phrasing is one more means toward that end.

There is little the young performer intent upon a stage career can learn from the huge available mass of popular recordings. In particular, contemporary singer/rockers cannot act as role models for those who are concerned with a well-sung song. The high decibel count combined with language that is often unintelligible are not integral building blocks in a *singer's* art. This is not meant to imply that a good performer does not score within contemporary singing styles—only that he does so in a different ballpark.

Further: MOR vocalists tend to clone in imitation of those who have already caught the public's ear. Their "sound" does not recognize phrasing as fundamental to their style.

Further still: Soul and Gospel singing are delivered in yet another musical language. However, I recommend that the young musical theater performer study the passion and energy in the work of Aretha Franklin, Tina Turner, and the late, unforgettable Mahalia Jackson.

Still further: The work of the late Sarah Vaughan, Barbra Streisand, Tony Bennett, or Vic Damone offers less education than one may imagine, for it must be evident to even the most untutored ear that, for these singers, vocal opulence is everything. If you do not have it, you do not have it. This is not to say that these worthies do not phrase what they sing, only that no one really cares if they don't. If your inadequacy is vocal, it is to your benefit to turn your attention to the importance of the text of the song. Ideally you should be concerned with both. After all, the singer who "sings" with full throat and empty mind must forever be on the alert—someone right behind him may be able to make an even prettier sound.

And, finally: The great jazz vocalists (Ella Fitzgerald, Sarah Vaughan, Carmen McRae, Al Jarreau, et al.) are recommended if only because their excellence demands attention. But the composers and lyricists who write for the stage require a conservative presentation of their scores. After all, it is the first time the audience hears the songs. Variations on unheard themes would be counterproductive. Jazz vocalism owes its very essence to improvisation. In the musical theater, the word is anathema.

The next chapter focuses on auditioning, a venue in which the performer is called upon to present himself as a singular interpreter of the songs he chooses to sing. Since phrasing, either from lyric or from music, is very much like a fingerprint, it is a major contributing factor to his uniqueness.

I Promise You

4

The Audition

Respect all such as sing when all alone.
—Robert Browning

In *On Performing*, I have written extensively about auditions from both the point of view of the performer and of those who are auditioning him. The process itself is intriguing in that it brings two mutually exclusive units into confrontation. The performer is there, either on stage or in a room, to get a job by showing what he can do; sitting in judgment is the hirer who elects to buy or to bury. It is a creaky and impractical operating procedure since the performer may well be working at less than his optimal level of achievement (nerves, the pressure born of the need for the job, and the usual obstacles that auditions engender), while the judgment capabilities of the disparate arbiters "out front" can range from downright ignorance to a sophisticated and surprisingly knowledgeable understanding of what makes for a good, a mediocre, or a poor performance. But nothing more effective has ever been invented to replace the audition and we are all, on both sides of the line, stuck with it. If auditions really did first divide the wheat from the chaff, then the good from the better, and then make certain the best was hired, there would never be the whisper of a complaint from either corner. But the human factor forbids objective judgment of the work at the same time that it seldom permits an ideal presentation of the artist's skill. Great performances in musicals are rarely the result of sensitive detection of talent found hiding within the strictures of the audition system. More often, audiences see performers who have gained their employment through the recommendation of trusted middlemen or just plain luck. I have seen first-rate performers fail to intimate even a fraction of their ability at an audition, and, as a quondam hirer, I have been taken in by a singer whose audition advertised a gift for auditioning but who, during rehearsals, proved it was his only gift.

THE JUDGES AND THE JUDGED

Readings for a play tend to be more efficient than auditions for a musical. On the one hand, there are fewer judges—the playwright and the director, being only two in number, can confer easily—and on the other hand, the actor is reading material extrapolated from the script that will be going into production. It is worth noting that, although the producer may be in attendance, rarely will his vote affect the casting of the play unless he, too, is eminent enough to swing opinion. Of further note: The author, by right of membership in the Dramatists Guild, holds the final veto on all casting, but if he is young and the director is a heavyweight, he may have to bend to the will of the stronger power.

In apposition, auditions for musicals are Towers of Babel. To begin with, what is being sung has nothing to do with the score of the planned production. And where only two judges usually sit for the casting of a play, one may see an army in attendance to cast a musical, with everyone registering an opinion even when they do not have a vote. It is not impossible to imagine auditioning before the composer, the lyricist, the librettist (or two or three), the director, the music director (conductor), the choreographer, the choral director, the casting director(s), the assistants to each member of the creative team, and, if they are free to stop by that day, scenic designers, costume designers, lighting director, orchestrator(s), upper-echelon wives, and, of course, the producer(s). In the case of the latter, the number may be significant, depending on how many of them were required to amass the five or so million dollars at which today's musicals are budgeted.

Let me talk further about the judges before discussing the judged with equal candor. Though it might be contested, the truth is that few, if any, of the creative staff know anything about what they are witnessing at an audition. And fewer still can do it. The director of a play may very well have been an actor at one point in his career and can be expected to bring knowledge and compassion to the task of auditioning actors. This is rare indeed in the musical theater. I do not mean to imply that only someone who can sing, dance, and act is qualified to cast a musical, but a Zuleika Dobson ("I don't know anything about it but I know what I like") demonstrates an opinion that is no more valid than the next person's. It is my personal opinion that the game is played more fairly when the appraisal of a performance is made by a judge more or less able to do it himself. (NOTE: The deaths of Michael Bennett and Bob Fosse have robbed the musical theater of artists with this kind of expertise.)

Another harsh reality: I spoke of compassion because it is so often not in evidence at an audition. Appointment times assigned to the performer are ignored or delayed for more than an hour without an apology, thereby adding further to the auditionee's already abraded mental state; interminable waiting in the wings or in anterooms; interruptions early on, when "What are you going to sing for us?" could have been asked before the performer began in order to forestall displeasure and effect a change in the choice of the song; stopping the performer just before the end of the song when a moment or two more would have allowed the singer to complete the audition—all these are commonplace. Pianists supplied by the management may turn out to be inept and the singer can do little to protect himself from the assassination by accompaniment (see Chapter Sixteen: "Advice to the Songlorn," Held Opinions). And finally, callback after callback after callback may occur with the complicity of the performer, born out of fear that he will appear uncooperative and thus lose the job. (The Actors' Equity Association ruling allows for four callbacks, after which, if there is need for another, the performer must be paid one-eighth of today's minimum weekly salary of $740 for principal, or white-contract, roles in a Broadway production and $540 for the same roles in a bus-and-truck production. Needless to say, the auditionee never risks a confrontation with management.)

There are managements less guilty than others. There are directors and casting directors more knowing and compassionate than others. A true professional creates a climate in which the performer can function at his best since it is to the advantage of both parties to cast the musical as effectively as possible.

On the other side of the battle lines stands the performer who is no more a hero than management is a villain. I have written and helped cast musicals and I can testify that an endless line of third-rate auditions can erode the patience threshold of even the most sensitive writer(s), director, and choreographer. There is an appalling array of unqualified people who come on stage intent to prove that they do not belong there. This is more true of musicals than of plays, although I do not know why it is so. An odd footnote: The same actor who auditions for a play with apparent know-how and serious preparation will willingly run out onto a stage or into an audition room and sing a song he learned only an hour before and do it with no demonstrable skill whatever. Why is he disposed to do so overtly what he *cannot* do, and be unwilling to do, off the top of his head, what he *knows* how to do?

Uta Hagen, in her practical and passionate *Respect for Acting* (New York: Macmillan, 1973, p. 221), has this to say: "The profession of acting has been maligned throughout the ages. To a degree, we are to blame for this opinion.... In our longing for dignity, we have not followed through in our work to merit respect for our profession and respect for our own work in that profession."

The performer is often guilty of this same lack of respect for the musical theater. (I exempt the dancer because he is the most serious of artists and never stands accused of anything less than a total commitment to his work.) Only when he can perform sung material secure in the knowledge that what he knows, he knows and, more to the point, that it will be evident to those out front, can he justifiably attack the hirer and *his* tactics. If he gets the job he can only pray that the creative team, whose work has yet to be tested, will prove to be as craftworthy as he (see *On Performing*, page 22).

I have sometimes heard the auditionee blame a poor showing on the irksome circumstances and the disconcerting sensation of hostility that pervades the atmosphere of an audition. Although the "bad air" that lingers on a stage after hours of inferior performances may take the concentration of an Olympic contestant to neutralize, the truth is that a shattered ego seeks an escape hatch anywhere it can find it. Bad work is the consequence of inadequate preparation. Some degree of nervousness is to be expected when possible employment is at stake, but nerves and fear are not synonymous. We are frightened only when we do not know *what* we are doing and what we are *going* to do. Nervousness is not a destroyer. In its own way, it can be the unnervous performance that is deadly.

CHOICE OF MATERIAL

The eternal question, "What should I sing?" is integral to every audition. For our purposes, the question is better asked, "What should I *not* sing?" The following answers will help you make your choice, out of the infinity of published material, easier.

Eight *Don'ts* to Remember:

1. Don't choose a song that reveals your inability to sing it. Songs, like clothes, should accent your good points and help to dissemble your inadequacies. Shun those with vocal lines beyond your range (operatic arias and much of Andrew Lloyd Webber's and Stephen Sondheim's more classic scores), scripts that require a stunning dramatic projection (again, Sondheim in his *Sweeney Todd* mode), and lyrics that lay claim to your dancing ability ("Rap Tap on Wood," "[I've Got] Shoes with Wings On," and "I Want to Be a Dancing Man") when, in the course of their delivery, it is clear for all to see that you are nailed to the floor.

2. Don't choose a song that, when it is taken out of its original context, has nothing to say. "I'm Gonna Wash That Man Right Outa My Hair," deprived of soap and water, is an inanity.

3. Don't choose a song that, when taken out of its original context, loses its vertical importance. "Oh, What a Beautiful Mornin'," when performed on a sun-drenched staged, is a charming introduction to the world of *Oklahoma!* Its charm is considerably dimmed in the bleak and depressing amperage of a worklight.

4. Don't choose a contemporary song that you have fallen in love with after hearing it on a record until you have weighed its value away from your CD player. When the instrumental orchestration is replaced by a piano accompaniment, the song—and you—could very well be betrayed.

5. Don't choose a song that is currently enjoying great popularity or one that is an overexposed standard. Rest assured there will be sufficient renditions of both before and after your appearance. Fewer reprises—even by one—will be met with almost audible sighs of gratitude and relief.

6. Don't choose a song written by a friend or a member of your family. After all, it is *your* audition, not theirs. If a song is unknown to those for whom you are auditioning, there is considerable comfort in being able to say, when asked who wrote it, "Sondheim" or "Gershwin," rather than "my Uncle Harry."

7. Don't choose to sing a "signature song." You may hold the opinion that your rendition of "Over the Rainbow" or "People" surpasses Garland's and Streisand's, but why give anyone the opportunity to debate the point, or worse, measure you against the original?

8. Don't, if at all possible, choose a song written by the composer for whom you are auditioning. Like playwrights, they and their lyricists have strong notions of how they like their material sung. Yours may be an interesting variation but why risk dissent? On callback, however, you may be given a song from the score of the production for which you are auditioning. Here, the intention is not to hear whether you can *sing* but whether you can sing that *particular* song.

Two further *Don'ts* worthy of mention:

1. Do *not* make conversation. If you are spoken to, answer, of course. The exchange has probably been initiated in order to hear your speaking voice. But resist an effort to ingratiate yourself with a snappy "hello," a quick weather report, or an inquiry into the health of someone out front. This may seem a needless caveat but, in the grip of nervous jitters, you will be astonished by your gift for self-destruction.

2. Lastly, never audition without your own pianist. You will have easy rationales to justify any and every exception to this advice but, in the end, they are invalid. Your agent and/or the casting director will not only assure you that there will be a pianist for you to use at the theater, but that he or she is reputed to be another André Watts or Marian MacPartland. Don't you believe it. Even if it were half true, no pianist can be expected to be familiar with the specific accompaniment you require. It makes more sense to audition with a third-rate accompanist who knows your work than to sing with a first-rate one with whom you have never rehearsed.

Two *Do's*

1. Try your best to ascertain what the management wants to hear. Have your agent call ahead or, if you do not have representation, make the call yourself. The task of the writer(s) of the score and the director is made easier when, by your choice of song, you are in the country in which their work abides.

2. Dress for the part. I do not mean to suggest that you rent a costume or paint your fingernails green, but Sally Bowles in *Cabaret* will be harder for you to characterize and for them to visualize if you arrive in jeans or a basic black dress. Again, remember, they have a job to give and you are there to propose they give it to you. If you are given a callback appointment because your proposal has not fallen on blind eyes and deaf ears, do not muddy their memory of you and your work: Wear what you wore before. Don't change your hairdo. The purpose of the callback is to reiterate and recall what worked before. *Unless informed otherwise,* I suggest you even sing the same audition. It's a safe bet you must have done something right.

THE FLAWS WITHIN THE SYSTEM

Auditions are doomed to some degree of failure because there are always those who are more capable in a production than at an audition, and others who audition well and cannot perform half as effectively when the curtain rises. After all, an audition can be rehearsed and re-hearsed until it is merely that: a rehearsed performance. In that sense, the callback is a more reliable indication of the performer's skills.

A role may be given to someone who, when you see the final production weeks or months later, makes you wonder why A was given the part while B, C, or even D—all of whom auditioned for the management—were bypassed. Subsequently, you may even see B, C, or D play the role in a touring company or in summer stock theaters and have your opinion confirmed. Another flaw within the system.

Are there alternatives to the audition process? Few, unfortunately. It is always valuable (in musicals as well as in plays) when performers are brought to the attention of the hirer by way of recommendation. Someone on the staff may have seen their work and/or knows what they can do, or someone who may be aware of talent that would go unseen without recommendation brings the performer to the attention of the management. Because this happens more than you might suppose, I recommend a performer work wherever and whenever he can. You never know who is out front watching you. Being "caught in the act" is far more valuable to you than having to demonstrate your craft under the battle conditions of an audition—in an empty theater, lit by a cold worklight, or blinded by the glare of a "day lighted" room, alone and by yourself.

A successful audition is measured not by whether you get the job but by showing the very best that you can do—that day. The task of the creative staff is to cast the musical. Do not confuse the two. Factors outside your control condition their choices. There is no way you can outguess what they have in mind. If they are looking for a blonde, then a brunette, no matter how gifted, scores one out on entrance. If the in-genue or leading lady is tall, the juvenile or leading man must be taller still. If you are short, there is nothing you can do about that. An old show-biz joke tells of the agent's admonishment to a client on his way to an audition: "Oh, and for God's sake, watch your height!"

Of this I am certain: A good audition never goes unnoticed. It may not achieve immediate employment but no casting agent, composer and lyricist, or director ever forgets good work. There is too little of it.

5

The Song as It Reflects You

I celebrate myself and sing myself.
—Walt Whitman

The first moments in which the actor and the dancer begin to sing can only be described as a torment. The terror they feel can be awesome in its power to annihilate. As a teacher of the subject, I have witnessed every variation of stage fright from excessive perspiration to parched dehydration; from tremors to paralysis. An actress once confessed to me that even her hair was nervous when she first began to sing in class. She had quite literally felt it trembling. During the hours that a class is in session, checking out the comings and going to the restrooms gives a fair indication of who has just finished singing and who is thinking of singing next—adding loss of sphincter control to the list of aberrational behavior patterns that are triggered by the act of singing in public.

It may be no small comfort to learn that there is justification for this distress. The dancer's art is a mute one. Skipping over from speech to singing what he has to say can be traumatic. The actor is trained to surrender to and transmute into Hamlet, and his success is measured to the extent that he makes credible his disappearance behind that Prince's incarnation. So, too, the young Juliet and the aged Lear. During the course of the play who, in truth, is she? Who is he? We are destined never to know, for it is not alone their makeup but their art that dissembles their reality. However, unlike characters in a play, the songs we sing will not, can not and must not be hiding places behind which we find safe anonymity. *When one sings "I," one means "I."*

The performer is always visible above, below, and around anything he sings. It is our unconscious awareness of this that sets into motion the classic case of nerves that plagues us when we first stand up to sing ourselves. The neophyte feels he is as naked as a babe, convinced that his imperfections are visible to everyone. And he is correct in believing this, for great performing lives in the illusion of perfection—a world that does not recognize, or even see, defects. It can be argued that the art of great performing is manifest when the performer is more interesting than the songs he sings; the song less interesting than the singer who sings it. When a performance does not achieve this, the singer has either failed or he is singing the wrong song.

I offer a curious illustration of this phenomenon: Meet an actor whose work you admire and, more than likely, you are surprised by the disparity between him and your preconceived image of him. The dashing figure is a shy introvert. Miss M., the lady renowned for her charm when the curtain is up, is aloof and forbidding once the curtain falls. But meet a singer whose work you admire and your preconceptions are always confirmed. Garland was and "sang" Garland, Piaf was Piaf, Merman was Merman, and Lena Horne is Lena Horne. When we elevate what we have to say into the need to sing it, our true and unique essence is exposed.

In a *New York Times* interview, Harold Pinter remarked that speech " ... is speaking a language locked beneath it. That is its continual reference. The speech we hear is an indication of the speech we don't hear. It is a necessary avoidance, a violent, sly, anguished or mocking smokescreen which keeps the other in its place. One way of looking at speech is to say it is a constant stratagem to cover nakedness." Song, as soliloquy, is that "continual reference" to what we dare not speak, but are impelled to sing.

Another defeat suffered by the novice singer of songs: He cannot refrain from listening to himself sing. Most of us are shocked at the first hearing of our recorded voices and we are in no way assuaged by being told that, in the theater, audiences see a song more than they hear it. *We* hear it and our sense of inadequacy is more than enough to distract and destroy our concentration. In addition, when the actor first begins to sing, you can rest assured that his knowledge of acting will be forgotten and, under similar circumstances, the dancer will be unable to move. Even the singer, splashing through the simplest of subtexts, will fail to use his voice properly. In time of trouble, what one knows best appears to desert one first.

In the beginning, a number of revelations about singing support the performer and enable him to understand, if not easily endure, his torment:

1. It is somehow reassuring to learn that everyone suffers similarly. This is more discernible in a classroom, where he would be a witness to the symptoms of his disease in others, but if that experience is denied you, I pass it along as fact. In the shower, we sing full out and without self-consciousness not because we sing well but because we are alone.

2. Exempting the singer for obvious reasons, very little of what the actor or the dancer knows is of any value when he first begins to sing. There may be some superimposition of techniques at the end of the learning process but, at the start, each art is as disparate to the other as tennis is to golf. Again, the mechanism of fear is triggered when the ignorance is advertised in public.

3. Unless the actor has acquired a knowledge of verse (e.g., in the plays of the Elizabethans and the Greeks), speaking in rhyme and observing the rules of prosody are unique experiences. It makes little difference whether he performs "Yankee Doodle Dandy" or the most complicated Sondheim lyric. To speak (sing) in poetic, rather than prosaic, language is alien; the beginner performer may find himself feeling self-conscious and oddly foolish.

4. The lyric of a song is a sung lyric. It may be fractionally true that there is a melody in all language and sometimes "sung" dialogue may be put to the service of the text, as in the case of Professor Higgins when, by means of xylophone tunes, he teaches Eliza Doolittle to intone, "So kind of you to let me come." Admittedly, too, the "singing" may simply be a bad line reading but, in either case, the choice is made by the actor. But when he sings, his "sung" reading, the choice of the melody of the song is no longer *his* but the composer's.

5. The melody will be created on pitch levels far below and above what the actor uses in plain speech. If he is delinquent in the study of correct vocal production, he may well do himself bodily harm. The American actor is not known for the beauty of his speaking voice. His training focuses on what he considers to be more important aspects of his art. For someone who recognizes the difference between good and bad vocal production, listening to the constricted throat sounds produced by some of our more celebrated theater stars can be painful in the extreme.

6. The sung lyric is metered. Again, all language possesses an intrinsic rhythm. When that rhythm is sensitively communicated, language is the bridge over which the idea that birthed the speech is transmitted (see Chapter Three: Phrasing). Bad speech rhythms short-circuit that connection and the ensuing loss of clarity leaves the audience confused. Still, the actor can choose his rhythms, again with consequent good or bad results; he cannot do so when he sings. If the composer has set the lyric in the rhythms of a march, a march it is; if it is a waltz or a fast patter, he is a slave to that time signature. Resist the enslavement and he will receive some nasty notes from his accompanist or the conductor of the orchestra.

7. Nor is the actor *explicitly* cued. From the moment he begins to sing or, more specifically, from the moments before the moment he begins to sing, he has no reason to do so. No one is there to oblige him with, "What would you like me to do for you?" to make sane the singing of "Embrace me, my sweet embraceable you." He must learn how to create an *implicit* cue to replace the loss of the *explicit* one.

8. The actor is taught to live on stage behind the "fourth wall" (the invisible wall between himself and the audience), and the set gives credibility to his life. It must be Elsinore for Hamlet if it is to be Elsinore for us. But this does not hold true when he sings. A song does not live naturally behind the fourth wall. It stays there for little more than a moment after its birth and then seeks to move "down" and "out," unimpeded, into the theater. When, in the course of the production of a musical, it is forced to remain upstage, the performer must create his own thrust-power in order to make the song, as the French say, *passer la rampe* (go up, over, and through the fourth wall).

9. Lastly, the inherent subtexts that create phrasing choices and the demands of correct vocal production are intimidating to the novice. When their demands are addressed, they can do considerable damage to, and even preempt, his concentration on the performance of the song itself.

Further comments on the singer "singing himself": The actor who auditions will read from the manuscript of the play going into production (see Chapter Four: "The Judges and the Judged"). The musical theater audition begins with the classic question from out front: "What are you going to sing for us?" As described in the preceding chapter, the song they hear will not be from the score of the planned production but one the performer has chosen to approximate what he thinks they want to hear. By this act, the performer—whether actor, singer, or dancer—is forever defined. All singers of songs, from the very beginnings of their careers, choose their repertoires on their own or with the help of teachers, musical directors, personal managers, and anyone else whose input may have weight. The songs you hear on records, in nightclubs, on television, in concerts, and, to revert to that audition for a musical, are all the choice of the performer and not the hirer. (First and second callback auditions are rare exceptions since they may require the singer to learn material from the score of the musical for which he is auditioning. The problem of choice is solved: The performer has no need to guess what the hirer wants to hear).

The single responsible factor common to all failed auditions is traceable to ill-chosen material. This irrefutable fact may come as something of a shock but, nevertheless, it can be sobering to learn that you are counted out, almost immediately, not by your assets or your lack of them but by the liability incurred from an unwise choice of song. Why is the actor-singer not only unknowing and unaware of who he is but, even more, of how others see him? The answer is not difficult to come by: We are too often unmindful that, since things (and people) are seldom what they seem, those who witness our work have only what they see upon which to guage their judgements of us. It follows that we must learn the essential nature of our essence or essences—what it is we project from the stage—so that what we sing will never betray who we are and, of even greater importance, will appear to substantiate who and what those judges of our work *think* we are. In response to an interviewer's question about a possible conflict in his personal religious philosophy as it appears in his writings, Gore Vidal said: "But that's not for me to say, is it? Because I don't know; I don't see it. I'm inside the machine; you're outside it. You can observe—and what you find is more for you to see than me to say."

I am not speaking here of songs denied us by virtue of our gender. It would be a foolish man who chose to perform "The Man I Love" and an equally foolhardy woman who elected "The Girl That I Marry" as apt audition material. Nor do I allude to character traits that, for the purposes of this discussion, would be better consigned to a doctor's office for examination. But it must be apparent that we cannot all be acceptable singing anything and everything beyond those songs denied us by our conspicuous comportment and our gender. Just as a young juvenile would confuse if he sang "Silver Threads Among the Gold" and an aging character actress if she rendered "Young and Foolish," an effete young man dare not risk Leonard Bernstein's "Pass the Football" any more than someone overtly macho may risk Noel Coward's "Regency Rakes."

Remember, then: Songs have destructive powers—particularly the ones you choose for the purpose of gaining employment. Remember, too: Be aware of the hidden dangers in choosing a song simply because you like it and believe that to be of additional aid in performing it well. This is a misapprehension. What turns you on may not do the same for your audience. More than likely it will engender in you cheap emotional responses that, in turn, distract you from an intelligent command over the material. Like the knowing actor who shuns "results," the wise performer is concerned with conducting the emotional responses of his listeners. His task, like that of everyone in show-business, is to keep the audience awake and engaged. That is his objective—the *why* he is singing the song. Another point in favor of shunning songs you like to sing: It is more than likely that there will be times in your professional career that you will be paid to sing songs for which you do not care in the least.

There is no gainsaying an audience's pleasure in sensing and being affected by that special joy revealed in a singer's vocalism. Garland yearning to fly "over the rainbow," Sinatra doing it his way, Streisand's bottomless supply of breath lavished on a single vowel, Lena Horne's complaint that it "keeps rainin' all the time," and Tony Bennett's open-throated love letter to San Francisco—the list, fortunately for all of us, is a long one. Unfortunately for the actor and the dancer, only singers come to mind as prototypical. The point is that singers can *sing,* and when they sing well they take pleasure in making music. For those who do not possess a superior vocal sound, it is important to understand that singing is, quintessentially, a *doing* and not a *feeling* act. This is not easy for the actor, trained to codify the spectrum of his emotions, to accept. It is all too tempting to forget that the audience can be expected to react to music without emphasizing its emotional content. Worse, "feeling" responses can play havoc with one's vocal technique by closing the throat and demolishing breath. A simple rule: To get the audience to react with their hearts, you must learn to use your head; to know that what *you* do with a song will always be a statement peculiar to you alone. It will clothe you, but you must never allow it to hide you or to muddy your image.

In a play, the actor builds the character of another person, in another time and place and situation—one who will be manipulated by the events of the drama. But this does not happen when he sings. Now he is alone and, through music (an emotional language of preternatural size and importance), he will sing of what *he* thinks, what *he* feels, what *he* intends. It follows, then, that *what we are to the audience is what we seem to be* and, no matter how we may protest this unfairness, they—and our auditioners—will not and cannot be expected to forgive us our flaws. Since each of us, by virtue of our humanness, is flawed, that forgiveness must first come from ourselves. By recognizing that you will be seen as you appear to be, the clever choice of song will serve you as advantageously as the cunning choice of what you choose to wear.

Diane Arbus, the late photographer whose camera was drawn toward images of human beings at the far edge where the ordinary becomes extraordinary, said about her work: "It is impossible to get out of your skin into somebody else's. Everybody has this thing where they need to look one way, but they come out looking another way, and this is what people observe. You see someone and essentially what you notice about them is flaw. Our whole guise is like giving a sign to the world to think of us in a certain way but *there is a point between what you want people to know about you and what you cannot help people knowing about you.*" (The italics are mine.) It is at the point when the singing of a carefully chosen song, whether you like it or not—both the notion and the song—can direct attention to one side or the other of that line of demarcation Miss Arbus speaks about.

Emerson's suggestion, "Use what language you will, you can never say anything but what you are," is most relevant when you sing. Even if change were advisable, it is too late to effect it beyond the simplest of acting adjustments. The actor-singer must learn to stand on the stage without a role to play, undiminished in his own skin. He must know the extent of himself—his height, his width, his depth; he must be aware of the ends of himself (his hands and feet) and the amount of air he displaces. And he must recognize that this displacement of air is as specific as the water he displaces when he lies in his bath.

A GAME: THE YOU NOBODY KNOWS

I like to play a game called "Essence" at the beginning of the classes I teach. Each actor stands on the stage and, one at a time, sings the same song. (I am partial to Rodgers and Hart's "Where or When" for three reasons: 1. everyone knows the melody, even unconsciously; 2. the lyric is easily dictated and memorized; and 3. the song is a cool, objective statement that precludes excessive emoting.) When he is finished, the class and I offer quick, subjective adjectives that describe our immediate reaction to what we have seen. No time is given for a slow, considered assessment because no slow, considered assessment will be made of him at an audition. The subjective nature of these reactions is of great importance to the performer because they are evaluations made by strangers, and strangers can be expected to be his future assessors. Although we know that what meets the eye may not be so, we are powerless to resist erroneous snap judgements, any more than the auditioner can inhibit them. Auditions begin and end within a time span of minutes. How often, when we are on the receiving end of "Thank you very much" or "We'll call you if we need you," would we willingly sell our birthrights to be able to ask, before exiting, "Uh ... I wonder ... would you ... uh ... please tell me what you saw? What you honestly thought of my work? Why you don't care to buy it? ... and ... please ... don't spare my feelings."

By defining for the actor what we saw as he stood there sing-ing—and drowning in nervous self-consciousness—I am attempting to fulfill that Walter Mitty fantasy in as constructive a manner as I can. It is the last time the class and I will be able to perform this function. As the weeks go by, the eye of love will begin its act of forgiveness and, by so doing, pollute our ability to see clearly what is not actually there to see. In possession of these qualitative and descriptive adjectives, I assign a song that, by its statement and musical texture, is the antithesis of the sum of the actor's essence, pushing into the foreground what is reces-sive and placing in shadow that which is dominant and possibly de-structive to him. For those who will be using this book with the help of an accompanist or a coach, the same principles should guide you in choosing a "wrong song." *Remember:* The technical exercises that are described in the following chapters are *not* designed to interpret the song but to be superimposed on it. Later, when you begin to perform the songs you *should* sing (the "right song"), this prosthesis will not be necessary. You will then be "singing yourself" but, at that point, you will choose acting adjustments that are not redundant to the essence and the text of the material. The effete young man may never sing "Pass the Football," but he will be wise enough not to add shades of lavender to "Regency Rakes."

6

Alert Warnings

Je commence encore à zéro.

—Edith Piaf

Each of the technical exercises that appear in Chapters Seven through Fifteen is to be executed on that *wrong song* I have described and, like a juggler who works with one, then two, then three and more balls, each is to be added to—and not a replacement for—the preceding ones. Do not expect facility early on. What will feel awkward at the start will seem less so with practice. I have said that singing is more an act, a thing *done* rather than something *felt*. The purpose of this technical work is to bring the actor down to his most simple physical condition ("zero"). It will introduce you to things that you will be asked to do or, more to the point, *not* to do. Think of it as a personal blackboard that must be erased and cleaned before you can write on it intelligently.

The beginner actor-singer is only too aware of the physical discomfort that causes his hands and feet to freeze or to behave in a kind of semaphoric insanity. This self-consciousness does not occur to such an extreme degree when he is acting—a further indication that singing what one has to say brings into play a different set of ground rules. Now, as he sings, he will be made aware of his physical life, to command a sane control over the four quadrants of his body. Physical statement is a significant element of performing but, for now, it will be absent. We are hell-bent, at whatever the cost, to vocalize the music while learning the disciplines that are concerned with *doing nothing*: not a twist or a tremor, not a jerk or a shake, no listing to port or to starboard, no twitching fingers, no eyebrows and shoulders duplicating the rise and fall of the melody, no rigid hands, no tilted head or bent knees, no slouching or toe-tapping, no empty or rolling eyeballs, just ... nothing. At this point, you will come to think of nothing as more than enough of a something.

Although "zero" connotes a complete lack of physical statement, it does not imply a death. In isolating the sensation of zero, there is no need to go below zero. There must be a continuing life-force whose energy forestalls paralysis.

"Zero" should not be considered an aesthetic aim (although there is a beauty of sorts in doing nothing well), but it does have a marginal advantage when you are asked to perform a lyric that is as complicated to receive as it is to deliver (an example is Sondheim's "Getting Married Today" from *Company*, when it is sung in the rapid-fire tempo the composer prefers). Here, a barrage of empty gesturing would murder the singer as well as the song. Given a choice of looking or listening, an audience can always be relied upon to take the path of least resistance. Along with clear articulation, an absence of physical language will guarantee that the message will be heard and even understood.

Do not mistake these exercises for a performance of the song. Think of them only as technical elements to be superimposed on the song. Stanislavski has said, "Technique is only of value on the stage when you forget all about it" (from *Stanislavski on Opera* by Constantin Stanislavski and Pavel Rumyantsev. New York: Theater Arts Books, 1975, p. 66). But technique must be mastered before you are able to forget it. Further, the demands of technique must be accepted unequivocally. There is very little sense to it at the beginning of a study experience. "Why?" has only its correlative "because." The dancer's barre work, the pianist's battles with Czerny, the singer's scales and melismatics, and the actor's improvisations must never be confused with *Swan Lake,* a Mozart piano concerto, *La Bohème,* or *Macbeth.* But you will come to know that technique, for all its constricting, is the imprisoning means to liberating ends.

Don'ts

1. Don't seek your comfort in these exercises. Your motor system is learning new coordinations that will be computerized into habit patterns in due time. Until then, you may very well feel *un*comfortable.

2. Don't seek relaxation if, by that word, you mean a loss or lack of tension. And do not mistake tension for tenseness.

3. Don't resist the feeling that you are in a kind of jail. You are. Move into the cell, hang some pictures on the wall, and make it your home away from home—for just a while. The sentence is not for life. Once you give up resisting, you will be astonished to find how much freedom is to be found in a prison cell. First ask yourself, "Am I doing this correctly?" If not, be certain you know why, and then fix it. If it is correct, don't be disturbed about how well you are doing it. With repetition, you will do it better.

Do's

1. The technical work that follows should be performed with a real sense of risk. Learn to dare to do what is asked "full out" and even larger than life. You can always make smaller what is too big. The reverse is by far more difficult to do.

2. Do keep a sense of humor about the work and about yourself. Singing is not the neurotic act you may think it is. When you finally learn to stand in the very center of the songs you sing, you will not have known a greater joy.

7

The Entrance and the Vamp

"Ready" is the password before Aim. My past is ready
not to intervene if I stand out of the way.
—Paul Goodman

IN THE WINGS

Actor-singers have to be disabused of the notion that, at an audition, it is their work alone that is being judged. Not that the quality of your singing and the presentation of what you have chosen to sing are not major factors. They are. But there is a third element of equal importance that has the power to diminish a positive reaction to them and that is, in no small part ... you, and how you come on, in both the literal and idiomatic definition of the term. Minds are made up all too quickly from the moment you enter onto the stage or into a room; how you react if spoken to and, still more difficult to accomplish well, how you comport yourself when no one speaks to you and you are left to live in a world of deafening silence; how you cue in your accompanist and how gracefully you perform the vamp that is the result of that cue and, when the vamp is finished, how you fill the silence with a song.

It is my opinion that anyone who can execute an audition with ease and maintain control over its proceedings has sung under battle conditions that make all other occasions seem like picnics. It is for this reason alone that I suggest that, when you work on the exercises that follow, you try to duplicate, in your imagination, the heightened atmosphere generated by the audition process.

To begin with: let us imagine that you are in the wings or in a room adjacent to the one in which you will be auditioning—and you are waiting. Waiting, as a subject unto itself, could fill its own chapter in any book about acting and/or singing. Waiting by day; waiting by night; waiting in the wings, waiting in your dressing room; waiting for a cue; waiting for an agent to call—waiting for it all to happen. In no other profession is time so wastefully squandered. And an audition is a paradigm of this waiting. Many are the times that you will be at the appointed place and assigned hour only to be told that you will have to wait. Backlogging delays are as integral to an audition as they are to a doctor's appointment schedule, and there are no back-number issues of *Time, People, Fortune,* and *Sports Illustrated* to make the waiting tolerable. (See *On Performing*, The Audition Process, for further relevant information.)

Don'ts

1. Don't fill the waiting time with idle chatter. Should you meet acquaintances in that decompression chamber between the street and the stage, make it clear to them that conversation is inimical to you. A haphazard backstage meeting must not be interpreted as a social encounter.
2. Don't give credence to backstage gossip. People can be thoughtlessly devastating when they tell a short brunette that they have heard "they're looking for a tall blonde." Just as it does in the army, a latrine rumor belongs in the room that gives it its name.

Do's

1. Use the waiting time to your advantage concentrating on what you plan to do. Nervousness may not be completely erasable, but it can be diminished when you do not spend the time thinking only about yourself. Go over the lyrics. Repeat your phrasing of them. Think of this moment as the first performance of the song and the one that will be presented "out front" as the second.
2. Center and quiet yourself. This may not be easy to do, but even the fractional effort you make to separate yourself from real and imagined distractions will work in your favor.

3. When this impacted life force has been created, you may enter. (This is a technical exercise. At an audition, your entrance is the consequence of hearing your named called.)

EXERCISE 1: THE ENTRANCE

1. Move to the optimal placement where the audition staff can best see your work. In the theater, it is and always will be: center stage. This cross from wings to center (or an entrance from an outer room) must be performed with your focus *off the floor*. Train yourself to think of this *consciously*. As you walk, work front so that you can more readily be seen and, as you go, take the measure of the *"space"* you will be working in. These positive tasks will be more profitable than the negative reminder: "I must not keep my eyes on the floor." This will be difficult to do. Every time self-consciousness, ignorance, false humility, constraint, or indecision (all the demons that possess us when we put our work and, more disquieting, ourselves on the line) intrude on your concentration, your eyes will drop and betray you. Your only defense is to stay alert and avoid the luxury of a blackout.

2. You are now standing in center stage or wherever the "hottest" placement may be. On a stage this geography will be more evident than in a room. (At an audition, center stage is as "hot" as the dismal amperage provided by the work light.) In either case, be motivated by sound theater principles: Where lighting is minimal, stand where it is least unflattering. If you are in a room where light is not a problem (daylight, after all, is daylight), stand not too far from and not on top of those who are auditioning you. Gaston's after-the-fact revelation in *Gigi,* " ... have I been standing up too close or back too far?" is not irrelevant. Most often, if a justified uncertainty exists, where to stand will be indicated to you by either the stage manager or someone on the staff. If that is not forthcoming and you are still confused, ask. No one will hold legitimate confusion against you.

3. You are now facing front. The more sensitive auditioner can be relied upon to institute a short exchange of small talk (name? history? credits?) that allows him to hear your speaking voice and, too, eases the atmosphere and makes possible a more honest demonstration of your work. However, do not expect this sensitivity to be guaranteed you. More than likely you will be met with silence and, in that case, I teach the following: When silence is what you get, do not make conversation.

Don'ts

1. Don't congeal. Resist the urge to stiffen at attention. Be "at ease" by putting your weight on one or the other side of the body. To prevent petrification I recommend devising some arm activity, but dissembling its mechanics. Study what your hands do under less extraordinary circumstances and use the information here. A bit of clothes-straightening, an easy hair-fix—your aim is to project a *living* presentation of yourself. Don't hesitate to linger on this self-physicalization. Out of too much you will select what you can use when you are working under real battle conditions. Don't be concerned if the exercise feels mechanical. Inevitably, you will find a sense of your ownness, and there will be no need to simulate a life—because you feel alive, you will be alive. Until then hold off death even if all you can invent is the illusion of life.

2. Although the actor in his dressing room before the play is not yet Hamlet, it is incontestable that he has already begun his journey into the character. Similarly, although there is interior preparation relative to the song you are going to sing, don't permit it to be seen on you. It is *you* standing there and, in this exercise, it is you *without a song.*

3. That "you" we see should be presented without additions and subtractions. Favorite inventions: amiability and the ready smile. Give them up. Someone once said that when you try to make an impression, the chances are that is the impression you make. In the theater, as in all professional venues, it is good work that purchases affection.

4. In the moments that precede the vamp, remember to keep a general focus. *Look* everywhere and *see* nothing in particular. Do not fixate on any one place in the theater or in the room. If you do, people will turn around to see what you are staring at. Now is the perfect time to check out the space and to measure its width, height, and depth.

Do's

1. On a stage your general focus—sometimes referred to as the "trajectory of the eye"—should be no higher than midpoint of the orchestra section. You will then be seen at your least provocative—neither too high nor too low. An interesting observation: When you feel comfortable with the height of your focus you can be sure that you are probably working too high. This is because you are doing what is natural—singing eye to eye to the theater. But, remember that you are *standing* on a stage, above those who are *sitting* out front. "Eye to eye," to them, will look like you are singing to the mezzanine.

However, in a room where a mezzanine and/or a balcony is patently *not* there, an eye-to-eye focus level is ideal. Since your auditioners are sitting on the same floor you are standing on, you will appear to be "spotting" just above their heads. If the auditioner is visible to you, you may, before a Vamp, recognize his or their presence—after all, they are sitting there and are a part of the world of reality. But once the song begins, *never* work to those who are auditioning you. Their function is to cast the musical and not to react to your performance. In either case, whether you work on a stage or in a room, inhibit the natural tendency to work too far north. Play it safe—bring your focus level down.

2. Further, focus that is too high will risk another kind of confusion for those out front who are watching you work. Whether the song you sing is meant for the theater-at-large (identified by the word "you" in the lyric when it implies "you-all," see Chapter Seventeen: "Focus") or the stated *you* is intended for only one person (e.g., Cole Porter's "I Love You"), in the former case, it is not to the gods you are singing and, in the latter example, save working *to* God if and when you sing "If I Were a Rich Man" from *Fiddler on the Roof.*

We are now at the point where we are ready to sing but, before you can do so, there is one mechanical act you must perform: *the nod* to your accompanist that cues in the instrumental vamp, without which you could not function (see Chapter Two: "The Vamp"). The nod is only necessary at an audition. During the performance of a musical, the music director knows at what moment the orchestra is to play. You will never be required to cue in the conductor. In nightclub acts, in television variety and talk shows, and in all situations in which the singer requires the accompaniment to begin (always, by fiat, before the actual vocalization), adequate rehearsal has taken care of the "when-to-start" moment. But at an audition, it is you who decree the "ready ... get set ... go." The nod, by dictate of custom, is the prescribed method that tells your pianist to ... Go!

EXERCISE 2: THE VAMP

In Chapter Two, "Air" was identified as music, within the body of the song, that is not sung. In the order of importance, the Vamp was named the number-one "Air" pocket. There are strong reasons for this.

1. It is the first music heard and it signals the imminent arrival of the first words of the song.

2. It has a built-in inevitability factor, namely, it not only seeks vocalization but is guaranteed to end when the performer utters the first

vocalized note. (No singer asks for a vamp and, at its conclusion, decides not to sing.)

3. Because it represents the prenatal life of the song, how the singer shapes the evolution of this inevitability is an indication of the grace of his style.

The length of the Vamp is always determined by the relative *weight* of the script and the *height* of its first line. (See Chapter Two: p. 24.) For the purpose of this series of exercises, I suggest a four-bar Vamp as the sufficient length of time in which to perform what will be required.

Let us admit from the start that the act of singing what you have to say is absurd. Only the audience's willingness to accept it as normal behavior gives it its sanity. A collective-unconscious understanding has existed since the beginning of recorded history (and probably before then) between the singer and the auditor, one that, by virtue of the power of music, makes acceptable the conversion of speech into song. But theater music truly strains credibility. Sung out of context, it has only its Vamp to push it from the horizontality of speech into the verticality of song. If you think of that Vamp as the gantry that props up and sustains the missile (the song) before it is launched, you begin to see the importance and the strength of the Vamp's thrust power. The length and the timing of it is nothing less than the countdown before the blast-off (the first bar of vocal music).

Another consideration: When a performer sings a song that is extrapolated from the score of a musical, that song can be said to have been surgically removed from its placement in the libretto. A scene(s) has not only preceded it but also given the song its specificity as well as its vertical height. At an audition, it is deprived of these and yet the song struggles, in some mysterious way, to retain them. Using *"My Fair Lady"* as an example: at rise of Act One, Scene 1, Professor Higgins sings:

Look at her, a prisoner of the gutters:
Condemned by ev'ry syllable she utters.
By right she should be taken out and hung
For the cold-blooded murder of the English tongue! ...

Segue to:

Why can't the English teach their children how to speak? etc.

("Why Can't the English?" music and lyrics by Frederick Loewe and Alan Jay Lerner, from *My Fair Lady*, 1956. Copyright © 1956 by Alan Jay Lerner and

Expository and, therefore, informational, this lyric is unmistakably objective, intended for everyone to hear. In the context of its verticality, it can be said to be *low* off the floor. Only a short Vamp is needed to give it sufficient thrust. Two and a half hours later, the "eleven o'clock" song (a most subjective statement) is sung by the same character: "I've Grown Accustomed to Her Face":

Damn!! Damn!! Damn!! Damn!!
I've grown accustomed to her face!
She almost makes the day begin ...

Segue to:

I'm very grateful she's a woman
And so easy to forget;
Rather like a habit one can always break
And yet,
I've grown accustomed to the trace of something in the air;
Accustomed to her face.

In this perfectly realized lyric, Higgins's self-revelation occurs at the same time that it is revealed to the audience. The song has enormous elevation. In the performance of *My Fair Lady*, it inherits that height from the unreeling of the entire script and score, but in an audition that script and its unforgettable score are denied the performer. However, the song will be impelled to seek its height, even if it must be reached within the mere four, six, or eight bars of its Vamp!

Aware now of the integral importance of the Vamp, we can return to the mechanical act that brings it into being: the nod to your accompanist.

Don'ts

1. Don't smile your accompanist in. Whether he is a friend, an acquaintance, or even (as may be likely when you hear him play) an enemy, it is far too late to throw yourself on his mercy by adding an amiable nod to the fee you will pay for his services. A simple and visible down and up of the head gets it all started. Subtlety should be shunned. Two nods, as in the case of two Bell-tones, are pitiable.

2. Don't signal until you are ready to begin. That pianist is going to play when he sees you nod because he is so instructed. Beware. Even a moment too soon may well find the song singing you.

3. If the accompanist cannot see your nod, you must take more drastic action. Sometimes, he may be behind you. Turn around and cue him in. Sometimes he may be in the orchestra pit where he will be unseen and, unfortunately, not easily heard. Move down to the apron and make your contact. If a wave would be more visible, then wave him in. I have said that an audition is much like running an obstacle course. The winner is the one who copes best with whatever barriers are placed in his way. On the bottom line: *You* need the Vamp and *he* needs to be told when to start playing it.

4. Don't register any reaction when he begins to play (after all, you did nod); no rapid acting adjustments that give you the appearance of St. Joan hearing her "voices"; no hypnotic fixating on the pianist out of a fascination with his keyboard artistry. Remember: *He* is accompanying *You*. When the work of the pianist takes precedence over that of the performer, your failure is nothing less than total. I have known accompanists who secured employment in the very musical for which the singer was auditioning: total failure doubled.

Do's

1. After nodding and hearing the Vamp begin, wait a beat or two before taking your attention off the accompanist. Then, relate easily back into the general theater, making sure that you retain your sense of reality. You are not yet to give a hint of the song you are going to sing. Were a film to be made of you just before the nod and after your return *front*, there would be no visible change in your demeanor. Resist the temptation of allowing the sound of music to affect you. You are going to sing but, as in acting, proceed from moment to moment. The moment for vocalizing—even the moment *before* that moment, has not yet arrived.

2. You will be hearing a four-bar Vamp to a ballad. (The slow tempo of a ballad gives you ample time to perform the technical tasks in the Vamp and the subsequent vocalization of the song.) The first two bars of the Vamp will be taken up with the moment or two you stay with the pianist after the nod and you return front—still maintaining a general

74

focus into the theater and an easy physical life. *At the top of the third bar:*

a. Move your focus to Center (straight front). By this act, you have made specific what was general. All songs should begin with a center focus if only for the reason that it is provocative to start them elsewhere.

b. As the eye recognizes center, the base (feet) that was in a "sitting" posture (weight resting on one side of the body) shifts to weight evenly placed on both legs. This is done by the simple act of picking up the leg you are not standing on and making a base in which both feet support the body equally. Be sure your base is neither too wide or too narrow. Around twelve inches should ground you and provide adequate support.

c. As your base moves into position, start your hands moving to your sides, one following the other.

3. As the fourth bar of the Vamp ends, your focus should be front and center, your weight planted on both feet, and your arms easy at your sides.

At this point, just as the song is ready to be vocalized, go no further. The first and second exercises (the Entrance and the Vamp) have been completed. Remember: The creation and recognition of the Center spot are always the primary acts that give the illusion that it and its personalization impel you to sing. Later, when you are performing songs rather than performing exercises on them, your body will have been trained to *respond* to what your eye *sees*. You will have learned never to sing without someone, or the illusion of someone, to sing to.

Review

Before proceeding, let us review the order of the activities in Exercise 2, beginning with the nod and ending with the fourth bar of the Vamp:

1. You are standing on stage or in a room, ready to sing. Your weight is either on the right or the left leg (that is to say, "sitting" on one or the other side of your body), your hands are away from your sides, intent on some simple physical activity. The object, of course, is to resist turning into a piece of lumber during the moments before you sing.

2. Nod to the accompanist to begin the Vamp.

3. After a moment or two, take your eyes off the pianist and return easily to a general focus front into the theater (or the room) in which you are working.

4. On the downbeat of the third bar of the Vamp, bring your focus into center and *see, specifically,* what you had been *looking at generally.*

5. Upon reacting to the center "spot," your base should move from its seated position to weight evenly balanced on both legs, with feet twelve to fourteen inches apart.

6. As your base comes to rest, your hands move, one at a time, to your sides.

ONE-SIDED DIALOGUES

In the simulated teaching dialogues that follow, only my voice (herein-after referred to as DC) can be heard. Directed at two students, one male and one female, their purpose is to isolate the most common errors and to explain how, like Topsy, these exercises grew.

His Work

Mr. G. is thirty-four, of medium height, dark-complexioned, with strong masculine features. A cultivated muscularity gives the impression that his persona, although effective, was invented to substantiate the "look" of him. These qualities, combined with an absence of humor, induces DC to assign him, as a "wrong song," Cole Porter's "Looking at You."

VERSE   I've gone afar collecting objets d'art
I know the whole game by heart
Why, Joe Duveen will tell you what I mean
'Twas I who gave him his start.
    (NOTE: Joseph Duveen was an eminent art dealer).
But, (Note the ubiquitous 'but' mentioned in Chapter One: "Words as
    Script.")
Since I looked, dear, in your direction
I've quite forgotten my art collection
To be exact, you simply prove the fact
That Nature's greater than art:
1ST "8" Looking at you
(A) While troubles are fleeing
I'm admiring the view
'Cause it's you I'm seeing
And the sweet honey-dew of well-being settles upon me.
2ND "8" What is this light
(A) That shines when you enter?

```
          Like a star in the night
          And what's to prevent 'er
          From destroying my sight
          If you center all of it on me?
BRIDGE    Looking at you
   (B)    I'm filled with the essence of
          The quintessence of joy
          Looking at you
          I hear poets tellin' of
          Lovely Helen of Troy
          Darling,
LAST "8"  Life seemed so grey
   (A)    I wanted to end it
          Till that wonderful day
          You started to mend it
          And if you'll only stay,
          Then I'll spend it
          Looking at you.
```

("Looking at You," music by Cole Porter, from *Wake Up and Dream*, 1929. Copyright © 1929 Warner Bros., Inc. Copyright renewed. All rights reserved. Used by permission).

Here, then, to corroborate DC, Mr. Porter's own words " ... It's the wrong song in the wrong style." The lyric is elegant, the rhymes and references are wise and, for Mr. G., less a call of the wild than of Wilde.

While he is waiting in the wings, preparing to make his entrance (Exercise 1), DC speaks.

DC

(To the Class)

"Looking at You" is AABA in form. (As explained in Chapter Two, the first two "8s" and the last "8" are the same musical theme [A], while the third "8," more commonly called the Bridge, or Release, is a new musical statement called [B].) The scoring of the melodic line of the Verse allows it to be delivered out of tempo. Mr. G., after nodding to the pianist, will receive a four-bar Vamp in ad lib. As a rule of thumb with no exceptions, all ad-lib Vamps should end with a *sting* (a sustained chord, with the starting note of the song to be sung given preeminence at the top of the chord). There is only this to say about a *sting*: Never sing on it. This is not easy to do since it can so easily be interpreted as a command to sing. To resist the temptation, train yourself to count a heavy three beats after you hear it before you begin to sing. The stillness these beats create can be supportive and even dramatically effective. Nothing commands attention more than silence. Ecclesiastes, 3:7, tells us that "to everything there is a time to keep silence, and a time to speak." The quiet that follows a sting is the time for silence-keeping.

But Mr. G. appears to be ready. At an audition or a performance of any kind, your entrance is dictated by others. In the execution of this exercise, it waits on your own sense of readiness. Upon seeing that Mr. G. is entering, DC can only mutter the time-honored musical-comedy cue line: "Ah, here comes Mr. G. now ... " Moments later, Mr. G. has reached center state. DC stops him from continuing the exercise.

DC
(To Mr. G.)

Would you make your entrance again? As you crossed the stage, you dropped your eyes more than once to the floor, a sure sign of self-consciousness and indecision. Also, from the moment you appeared, you were impelled to add a personality "fix" onto yourself, very much like the telephone voice that sometimes we are all guilty of affecting. Have the courage to enter and not make any adjustments to what is already an integer—*you*. You are presupposing that if you do not add something to the sum of you, we will see that something is missing. Just come on and leave yourself alone. You cannot sing until you experience yourself truly. Get rid of the camouflage. Rest assured that the song you are going to sing will cover you. Don't be afraid. Once you have experienced this figurative nakedness, you will feel that you have never been more clothed. I am reminded of Samuel Hoffenstein's short poem "Proem":

> Wherever I go,
> I go, too,
> And spoil everything.

> (From *Pencil in the Air*, Garden City, N.Y.: Doubleday, 1923; 1947. Used by permission.)

We can only guess how people perceive us because we are forever denied their point of view. Trust me. As your teacher, I see you with an objective eye. And what I see is a man superimposing machismo on someone so obviously not in need of it.

Mr. G. takes this with good grace. Before he exits to try his entrance a second time, DC congratulates him for his professionalism. A professional, among other things, learns to differentiate between criticism of him (judgments no teacher has the right to make) and criticism of his work. After a few moments of preparation in the wings, Mr. G. reenters and moves toward center stage. This time, keeping in mind the notes he received, he plays front and into the theater, his eyes do not short-circuit to the floor, and, thanks to a stunning effort to leave himself alone, the class is allowed to see a new, and truer, man.

DC

(To Mr. G.)

Very good! Stay within the margins of the exercise and watch your focus. You are working too far to the left and right. Narrow the aperture of your camera eye. You don't have to take in the boxes on the sides of the house. Stay alert! Your eyes look like you are going to sleep. Keep awake! Arm yourself with thought. Remember: A variety and a consistent rebirthing of thoughts, no matter how trivial, are more valuable than the quality of one thought which, as soon as it cools, leaves you empty-eyed. Shopping lists, logarithm tables—*anything* you put your mind to will keep you awake; *nothing* will put you to sleep. Good! Very good! Whatever you are using is effective. There is no need for the class or me to know what is on and in your mind—only that you be aware that, whatever it is, it is working for you.

Mr. G. is back on stage a few days later. Armed with the notes he received, his performance is much improved. The macho excess has been softened, his focus into the theater is less wide, and he generates an air of active wakefulness. DC is unstinting in his praise of Mr. G., who continues the exercise in center stage, seeking to keep his body alive, hands away from his sides, and his base in a "seated" position. DC edits further:

DC

(To Mr. G.)

May I speak about your hands? Like your feet, they are extremities, the endings of yourself. They not only have no minds of their own—they are furthest from the one mind they must obey. When that mind does not inform them, they are going to flap, flip, fluster, flutter, go up, go down only to go up again, shrug, shake, wave, and waver. In this exercise, before they come to your sides (and, in general, in the performance of all sung material), be guided by this simple, wise rule: Whatever your hands want to *say* or *do,* if it can be done lower, tell them—order them—to say or do it as *low* as it can be done on the body vertical. Hands flapping around your chest and face can and will upstage you. There will be enough battles in your career when you will have to cope with that murder. Why be guilty of committing it on yourself? Until your body knows what it is doing because it has been told *what* to do (at which point, it will have much that is valuable to say), we have to teach it good behavior. Before the Vamp began, you were keeping your hands away from your sides, as instructed. You chose, figuratively, to "wash them"—a good choice. But see what happened. Slowly they began to rise. As your elbows tightened, your arms moved still higher until you looked like Dickens's 'umble Uriah Heep. Bring your hands down even lower. No, keep washing them—but can you do it lower still? Good! You see, they are doing what they have been told to do, but by doing it as low as possible, they are now out of our line of vision. As a result, you yourself are more visible to us.

(To the Class)

Now, of course, you cannot pull at your ear, run your hand through your hair, or straighten your collar without bringing your hand or hands up, but those functions can only be performed at those body levels. The activity Mr. G. chose lost nothing by keeping his hands way down, and gained everything by giving them less prominence. Hands and feet wait for instructions. When those instructions are not forthcoming, they go ahead without them. There are a fortunate few who are blessed with a certain physical grace. Their hands move in elegant patterns that, although meaningless, are decorative. For those who are not so lucky, it is a good idea to train yourself, for now, to work at zero. By giving your hands nothing to say, they will be ready, later, to make their contribution to your performance. They will have much to say during the performance of a song, but until you learn the importance of that specific language, I ask you to train them to say nothing. The employment of the empty gesture is nothing but the advertisement of mindlessness. To quote Stanislavski: "Make out of every gesture some act, and in general forget about mere gestures when you are practicing. Action is all that counts. A gesture all by itself is nothing but nonsense." (Constantin Stanislavski and Pavel Rumyantsev, *Stanislavski on Opera.* New York: Theater Arts Books, 1975, p. 6.) Take my word for it. You will find it a good deal easier to make a good something out of a good nothing than out of a bad something.

(*To Mr. G.*)

Everything is now set for "go." Take a moment or two to get back on track, relate easily into the theater and, moving on, "nod in" your pianist.

(*To the Class*)

The work you are seeing Mr. G. do may not as yet be defined as good, but it is being done correctly. Soon, new habit patterns will be established and the exercise, instead of being done by Mr. G., will simply <u>be</u> him.

Mr. G., staying within the demands of the exercise and with DC's permission, nods to the pianist on his right. The ad-lib Vamp for "Looking at You" begins. Mr. G. brings his eyes to Center but before he can continue, DC stops him and the pianist.

DC

(*To Mr. G.*)

By going straight from the pianist to the Center focus you look like you are executing an "eyes-left" military maneuver. Instead, after you nod, stay with the pianist for a moment or two—then come back into the theater, but first linger somewhere a little to the Right of Center. Remember, you are not to spot Center until the top of the third bar. (If your accompanist is on your Left, this would be performed in reverse.) The timing of your arrival at Center should be gracefully executed and should not draw attention to itself. This can be effected by choosing that local stop closer to, rather than farther from, Center. In this way you will not jerk from Right (or Left) to Center. When it is time, just move your eyes easily to Center and then follow with your head. You would do just that under less self-conscious conditions. It is the simultaneous moving of your head and eyes that gives you that spasmic military look. (Breaking down the act of seeing into two counts will illustrate the sense of eyes first, head second. One recognizes with a follow-through of the head what one first sees with the eyes. Only those who are blind reverse that action. Deprived of sight, the head moves first as the ear seeks the source of the sound. The eyes, unseeing, follow, but only to seek the general location of what has been heard.) Now, after your arrival at Center, I want to believe that you are seeing what you went there to see. Blink! You look like you are working to a twirling half-dollar. The Center spot is hypnotizing you. By the way, there is no need for profound thinking. A simple but silent "hello" will do just fine. Also, you are pressing on the spot rather than seeing it. No need to insist upon the presence of the theater. It is there. It is not more there when you see it harder, or worse, play at seeing it.

(To Mr. G. and the Class)

Remember, focus achieves reality when you invest it with a life. It is not just a spot you are looking at but a life out there that you will be working to. What you use to make this anthropomorphic adjustment is of no concern to me or the audience. If it is a girl you imagine for yourself, fine. If a lamp shade affords you the same life, use it. What is important is that you are seeing someone (thing) and not acting seeing it.

(To Mr. G.)

Two more things to police: First, like your hands, focus tends to rise—as yours did when you came to Center. This has some psychological justification. You are getting ready to sing and at the same time you are making an unconscious effort to run away. Because that escape hatch is denied you, your focus seeks to reject the presence of the theater and rises. Bring it down. Also, the pianist seems to exert a magnetic force on you before you nod to him. It is as though you know he is there and this knowledge impels you to play almost exclusively into the Right of the house. But there is no pianist until you need him. You need no one. Furthermore, *during the moments preceding the nod to your accompanist, you do not even need a song.*

Mr. G. exits for the last time and reenters to perform Exercises 1 and 2 in their entirety. The work looks as though it were performed by the numbers but DC, as stated above, does not disapprove. It is a transitional moment in the learning process. The Entrance, the moments before the Vamp, the nod to the pianist, the return into the theater, and the easy arrival at Center at the top of third bar have all been attended to. As the fourth bar of the Vamp ends, Mr. G. is at attention, weight on both legs and his arms and hands are at his sides. When next we meet him, he will be singing.

Her Work

Miss B. is in her twenties. She is attractive and gifted, but DC and the class have noticed a disturbing tendency to inject feminist doctrine into any and all discussions, no matter its relevance. She is overarmed for the battle of the sexes. DC, determined to softpedal her air of benign belligerence, chooses for a wrong song, Rodgers and Hart's "He Was Too Good to Me."

VERSE	There goes my young intended
	The thing is ended
	Regrets are vain.
	I'll never find another half so sweet
	And we'll never meet again.
	I was a good sport
	Told him goodbye
	Eyes dim, but why complain?
1ST "8"	He was too good to me
(A)	How can I get along now?
	So close he stood to me
	Everything seems all wrong now.
2ND "8"	He would have brought me the sun
(B)	Making me smile
	That was his fun!
3RD "8"	When I was mean to him
(A)	He'd never say, "Go 'way now"
	I was a queen to him
	Who's goin' to make me gay now?
LAST "8"	It's only natural I'm blue
(B)	He was too good to be true.

("He Was Too Good to Me," music and lyrics by Richard Rodgers and Lorenz Hart, from *Simple Simon*, 1930. Copyright © 1930 Warner Bros., Inc. Copyright renewed. All rights reserved. Used by permission.)

Miss B.'s acceptance of the Rodgers and Hart assignment is not without struggle. With some justification, the sex-object songs churned out by Tin Pan Alley and the Broadway theater in the first half of this century are rejected out of hand by women who are the inheritors of the feminist revolution. There can be no gainsaying that Oscar Hammerstein's

I was created for one man alone
It wasn't easy to find
Now that I found him I wonder just how
I could have lived right up to now
Now I am someone completed by you
I am no one—just part of two.

(The Verse of "Don't Ever Leave Me" by Jerome Kern and Oscar Hammerstein II, from *Sweet Adeline*, 1929.)

are words the modern woman is not comfortable speaking. A further irritant: the lyrics were written by men for women to sing. As testimony to the vast generational culture gap: Holly Near's "Get Off Me, Baby":

Get off me, Baby
Get off and leave me alone (*repeat*)
I'm lonely when you're gone
But I'm lonelier when you're home.
Get off me, Baby,
You're weighin' my body down (*repeat*)
Your lovin' don't make me tingle
It only rolls me aroun'
I'd tell ya to go find another woman
But I'd hate to pass you on
That would be like passin' on to a sister
A pretty packaged bomb.

The work of Lorenz Hart presents a sad irony. Far from being the enemy, he may well have been the first lyricist to strike a blow for women's and gay rights fifty years before these words gained currency. The Bridge and last "8" of "Too Good for the Average Man":

Lots of kids for a poor wife are dandy
Girls of fashion can be choosy
Birth control and the modus operandi
Are much too good for the average floozy!
Psychoanalysts are all the whirl
Rich men pay them all they can
Waking up to find that he's a girl
Is too good for the average man.

Noel Coward claimed to have been born in a generation that still took light music seriously. That generation, the one that preceded mine, passed on to us this same regard for theater songs. The music of Gershwin, Kern, Rodgers, Berlin, Porter, Arlen, Schwartz, Youmans, and all the other contributors to that singular marketplace was collectively prized and afforded a very special kind of respect. It was a conditioning, along with its concomitant osmosis, that educated our sensibilities to pure melody. Even Tin Pan Alley's product, albeit more trivial, had to be sung. Crosby, Sinatra, Como, Bennett, Damone, Tormé, Fitzgerald, Vaughn, McRae, and Mercer, among many others, may have been disparate in personality and style but they shared one talent in common: They could sing. This singular element of the music in today's air has been denied those who followed us. There is much to praise in contemporary music but it has not contributed any significant melodic material to the collective American unconscious. It is my personal conviction that the nostalgia craze among audiences (and certainly among those whom I have taught) is traceable to a yearning for sheer melody —for it is melody that is the very essence of that historic body of *vocal* music. "He Was Too Good to Me" not only represents this genre but it is a beautiful example of the art of Richard Rodgers. It is simple and sumptuously singable. The sixth and seventh bars of the Verse include a shifting of keys in the melody as well as in its accompaniment that, once learned, is never to be forgotten. The music of the second and last "8s" has a vaulted vocal arc made lavishly open-throated by the particular vowels in the words assigned to the melody. All in all, it is irresistible, and Miss B. succumbs. Again, it was Mr. Coward who, in *Private Lives,* referred to the potency of cheap music.

She retires into the wings to prepare for her entrance, just as Mr. G. has done before her. Again, DC takes the opportunity to fill the silence with information about her song.

DC
(*To the Class*)

The Verse is in ad lib and, as in the case of Mr. G's song, it will be introduced by a four-bar ad-lib Vamp. The Chorus is ABAB, in thirty-two bars. In this song-form, there is no Bridge (Release). (See Chapter Two: Music: The Other Script.) The first and third "8s" have identical musical themes, while the second and last "8s" match with only minor variation.

Miss B. has witnessed the work of Mr. G. and does not require a recapitulation of Exercise 1, but DC interrupts her after her entrance. Her natural rhythms have propelled her out of the wings and into center stage as though pushed from behind.

DC
(*To Miss B.*)

There is no need to make an entrance faster, or for that matter, slower, than what would be described as normal. In your case, your rhythms seem hurried. Do not forget that you are being watched and studied from the moment you enter. Allow them the time to do what they are going to do whether you make their task easy or difficult. Also, from the moment you cleared the wings, your eyes went straight to a Center focus out front and waited there for you to join them. Here is an opportunity to take in the section of the theater to the right of you as you are moving from Right to center stage. In this way, you can see the part of the house you are leaving and, as you cross, pan the theater. (The word "pan" is used in film to describe the movement of the camera along the horizontal plane to achieve a "panoramic" effect.) By the time you have reached Center, your eye will have taken in the width and depth of the theater (or the room) you are going to work in. You should always be aware of the space you have to fill. Here is the perfect time to guage its margins.

Miss B. exits to enter again. This time her pace is slower and her eyes have taken the theater's measure, as instructed. She continues the exercise at center stage. Her arms are away from her sides and she is "seated."

DC
(*Again, to Miss B.*)

Let us take a moment to talk about your feet. Like one's hands, they are the great betrayers. This is why I ask the performer to work from the base up after focusing Center. If her feet were to move last, just before beginning to sing, the attention of the audience would be directed to the opposite part of the body from the one they should be watching. In your case, while you were in the "seated" position, the ankle of the leg that you were not standing on was what I call "broken." It is false, prettied up, behaving like a model showing off a dress.

(*To the Class*)

Fear is a virus that, given half a chance, attacks focus (the rolling eyeball syndrome) and the joints of our bodies. It short-circuits the current that should be flowing from you and the message you send out to the audience who, in turn, gives it back to you with its attention. Be alert. It is at the juncture of a joint—ankles, wrists, elbows, hips, knees—that this circuit is at its most vulnerable.

(To Miss B.)

I want to discuss choice of clothes only as they pertain to the theater and its imperatives. You are wearing white shoes. They are most attractive but, because they are white, I cannot take my eyes from them. It is unwise to wear them for an audition—unless you are prepared to dance, preferably tap dance.

(Again, to the Class)

When you are dressing for a job, stand before your closet with this in mind: What you choose to wear on the street and what you elect to wear at an audition stem from different motives and even, perhaps, from different closets.

Miss B. is eager to try the exercise again. This time, having been made aware of the tempo of her entrance, her focus is Right and Left into the theater as she crosses to Center, and in the behavior of her feet there is marked improvement. DC is extravagant in his praise and then, turning to the Class, summarizes the lessons learned from Exercises 1 and 2 before moving on to the next step: the singing of the song.

Both Miss B. and Mr. G. have submitted to the dictates of these first two exercises with grace. It is difficult for the actor to accept the peremptory direction that is characteristic of so much of the work asked of them in the technical sections of this volume. But, beyond the technique, there is a value to this *outside-in* manner of working. What is alien to the straight play is inherent to the musical theater. In the case of the latter, direction may consist of autocratic instructions. *Staging* and *form* may decree content. The rehearsals of a play comprise countless moments of discussion of character and psychology of intention, and this accretion of detail enriches the final texture of the piece. Contrarily, musicals are more mechanical in their structure. In rehearsals, time is the enemy. There are choreography and songs to be staged, music to be scored and scenes excised of all expendable dialogue, and there is very little time for discussion. Externalized *staging,* the bane of the serious actor's professional life, is not only routine, but an effective method for achieving the results that will finally be seen on the stage (see Chapter Seventeen: "Performance vs. Staging"). It is of inestimable value for the actor to learn how to live with the demands made on him by the director and the choreographer. Even when the direction seems awkward, or worse, false—do it. You cannot know what the director sees from out front. Of parallel interest, relating as it does to comedy (a major element of musical theater), is this extract from the essay

"Chaplin on the Set" by Penelope Gilliatt (in *Unholy Fools: Wits, Comics, Disturbers of the Peace,* New York: Viking 1973).

"Eventually the moves harden and become mechanical, which is what he wants. Once the routine is fixed and has started to bore the actors, the comedy begins to emerge. He works from the outside inward: first, the mechanics, then familiarity and physical skill, and after that, the right emotions will come. It is the diametric opposite of the Stanislavskian style that has become accepted modern dogma."

Interesting and often serendipitous results can be found in the journey the actor-singer takes during the rehearsal period of a musical. Exercises 1 and 2 and the tasks you are asked to do in the following chapters afford a small hint of that dictatorial climate. Go with it. You are gaining the experience that will enable you to deal, later in your musical-theater career, with the raised voice, the hysteria, and the rages directors are prone to send your way. Fear not—on opening night, with the arrival of glowing notices, everyone will become an instant and lifelong friend.

8

"Air": The Space Between the Lines

Don't just do something, stand there.
— A perversion of an intramural show-biz admonition

I have said that the great performer is always more important than the songs he sings; no song more interesting than the singer who sings it. When the reverse occurs, you have either chosen the wrong song, or, as you sang the right one, the "Air" became air pockets in the song. The work in this chapter, and in Chapters Eleven through Fifteen, concerns the basic concepts that will guard against these "drops."

To do battle with "Air" and to maintain your sense of altitude while singing through it, let us separate the three "how-to" divisions that are the parts of its sum:

1. how to identify it;
2. how to time it;
3. how to fill it.

WHAT IS "AIR"?

Identification is a simple equation: "Air" = music not sung within the body of the song. As previously defined, this music is found in the Vamp, in the spaces between the lines of the lyric (the music "fills"), and in the Rideout.

Exercise 2, in the preceding chapter, isolated the Vamp from the song proper and gave the performer an activity that would define the second half of the Vamp by physicalizing it. At its conclusion, the actor was brought down to a state of "zero" just at the moment before the first line of the song is born. Before moving on to Exercise 3, let us talk further about "Air."

It must be apparent that the actor-singer has no previous knowledge of "Air" because it does not occur in acting. In a state of dialogue, he speaks, and the end of his speech contains the cue words for someone else's speech. He may employ pauses to create meaningful spaces around the flow of the language but this is a choice *he* makes. It is not built into the script of the play. "Air" in a song is a fact of the music of the song. There is no choice. It is there as part of the mathematical structure of music and has nothing to do with the actor's decision to stop—or not to stop—the vocalization of the song. The "Air," then, is part of the game. The amateur status of the novice singer is apparent when he waits, with nothing on his mind, until the composer's "fills" are finished and he can continue with his sung monologue—the song.

The purpose, then, of Exercise 3 is to introduce the performer to the exact amount of "Air" (the mathematics of music) that must be filled before we can discuss the art of filling it.

EXERCISE 3: HOW TO TIME IT

Exercise 3 begins immediately following Exercise 2. You are at "zero" and the song is ready to begin. Only one adjustment has to be made at this point. Since you will be moving forward during each "air fill," if you are on a stage you will have to move *up* (back) at the finish of the Vamp. If you are in a room, move to an area where you can come forward unimpeded. In either case, remember: Do not lose the interior energy level that you were at when the Vamp ended.

The Vamp is finished, your focus is Center, your weight is evenly planted on a base neither too wide nor too narrow, and your hands are at your sides. You have begun to sing, using the Center focus, or "spot" as the specific *to whom* the song is addressed. When the first musical fill in the Verse arrives, you will define its length by taking *one step* forward (downstage). It is not important whether you stride with your right or your left leg, only that the second leg joins the first by making a base exactly like the one you were in *before* the step began.

Let me try to describe the exact timing of this move:

Q. When does the step begin?

A. On the downbeat of the last word sung before the musical "fill" (the "Air") begins.

Q. How long does it live?

A. Throughout the life of the air fill and into the first two or three words of the following sung line.

Q. When does it end in its new base?

A. Somewhere within the middle of the new verbal line.

The following lyric, "My Country 'Tis of Thee," is one we all know. I have chosen it for no other reason than to indicate the duration of the one air fill in it:

My country, 'tis of thee
Sweet land of liberty
Of thee I sing. (*Air*)
Land where my fathers died,
Land of the Pilgrim's pride
From ev'ry mountainside
Let freedom ring.

The step would occur between the words "sing" and end, in the new base, somewhere around " ... where my ... ," as illustrated:

91

Don'ts

1. In your eagerness to move, don't anticipate the arrival of the "Air" by leaving too soon. In the above example, that would be starting the step on the words " ... thee I" instead of on the "s" of " ... sing."

2. Resist the temptation to bring your second foot (the one following the stride) down to make the new base at the moment you hear yourself begin to sing. Again, in the example above: Don't end the step on " ... land" but continue its physical life into the new line, somewhere around " ... where my ... " By the time you are singing " ... fathers died" you should be standing in the same base you were in when you began, at zero—but one step further downstage.

Do's

1. Try to time the step smoothly. If there is a long musical fill, your step should be slower. If the "Air" is short, the move will be correspondingly brisker. The intention is to keep the step alive and moving as long as the musical arc of "Air" lives.

2. Take yourself with you as you go. Resist the tendency to tilt back or lunge forward while you are moving. Think of it as a "no frills" step. Its simplest execution is the most desirable one. The performer, translating his comprehension of "Air" into a move downstage, indicates that he is in control of both the concept (mental) and the execution (physical) of the technique.

DIALOGUES

His Work—The Character Actor

Mr. M., despite his years, presents himself as a younger man by dressing modishly in order to affect a youth he can no longer claim. DC is powerless to alter the conspicuous truth. The character actor, by virtue of his appearance, is denied the observably wrong song. One cannot change what is a chronological fact. At an audition, the given is that the character actor is there to sing and to read for the character role. Categorical casting, so much a part of the musical theater, does not permit too radical a *fix* on what the eye sees. The wrong song, then, now deals more with what the ear hears. DC chooses Arthur Schwartz and Dorothy Fields's intimate confessional, "Alone Too Long," for Mr. M.

VERSE If I seem to be shy and slow to hold your hand
　　　　It's because we're face-to-face this way

And there's so much I'm afraid to say. (*Air*)
Could I tell, if I tried, the hundred things I planned?
Could I somehow feel you'd really understand? (*Air*)

1ST "8"   I'd kiss you if I dared
(A)   I want to, but I'm scared
I should have known I've been alone too long (*Air*)

2ND "8"   My lips are much too still
(A)   My arms have lost their skill
My charm has flown,
I've been alone too long (*Air*)

BRIDGE   It's been years since I have whispered a foolish love-word
(B)   And I'd be afraid
I'd sing you a faded song (*Air*)

LAST "8"   But if you smile, and then
(A)   Say, "Darling, try again"
I'll know you've known
I've been alone too long.

Mr. M. goes to the wings to prepare for his entrance and performance of the Vamp (Exercises 1 and 2) and, in addition, Exercise 3.

Again, in the case of "Alone Too Long," there is an ad-lib Verse. The Chorus is AABA and the "Air" is marked so that the reader may know in advance when Mr. M. will be moving downstage.

DC

(*To the Class*)

This song boasts not only Schwartz's charming way with a ballad but offers the performer one of Miss Fields's most sensitive lyrics. Her work was notable for its romantic elegance without recourse to sentimental cliché. "The Way You Look Tonight," "Lovely to Look At," "I'll Buy You a Star," "Make the Man Love Me," "I Can't Give You Anything But Love," "On the Sunny Side of the Street," "Close as Pages in a Book" are all from her pen, as are the lyrics for the entire scores of *Sweet Charity, Redhead, A Tree Grows in Brooklyn, By the Beautiful Sea, Seasaw,* and, with Jerome Kern, *Swing Time,* arguably one of the best of the Astaire-Rogers film scores. But, it seems Mr. M. is ready ...

His entrance has profited from witnessing the work of those who went before him. DC asks him to move upstage while still playing into the theater. He does so, cues in the accompanist, and, with a Center focus arrived at in the middle of the Vamp, his weight on both legs, and arms at his sides, he starts to sing and even accomplishes his first downstage step in the "Air" between " ... I'm afraid to say ... " and " ... could I tell, if I tried ... " DC interrupts.

DC
(To Mr. M.)

Try that step again but this time do not think of it as simply a change in geography. True, you are moving downstage but if, as you go, you think of it as an elevation, you will experience how "Air" heightens the sense of drama as the song evolves. It is the element in the music that supports the song's continual escalation. Seven-league boots are not what you need. You could gain the effect I'm asking for by placing one foot directly in front of the other. It is not just the step you take but the tension within the move that you want to feel.

(Again, to the Class)

The semantics that distinguish *tension* and *tenseness* can be confusing. Tenseness implies the negative state of strain. It is inimical to both acting and singing. Tension, on the other hand, as used here, is the positive condition of harnessed potential energy. There are many words in the actor's dictionary that do not apply to singing. *Comfortable*, *relaxed*, and *improvisational* have no value for the singer. The act of singing is rarely comfortable, seldom relaxed, and never improvisational (unless it exists in a jazz environment). The extraordinary facility for scatting that is Ella Fitzgerald's trademark may be said to be ad libbed, but even she is imprisoned within the harmonic structure of the song. In the musical theater, lyrics, the music to which they are allied, and the accompaniment that supports their vocalization are something else again. There are too many people who are involved in the performance of a score to risk the slightest swing away from what has been "frozen" before the performance on opening night. If "relaxation" creates a state in which constriction cannot occur, I embrace the word. But with very little effort (no pun intended) relaxation alters into dangerous cognates like *ease, repose,* and *leisure*—words that are enemies of high-wire performing.

Mr. M. tries the Vamp and Verse again but not before DC tells him to cut the entrance from the wings. Once the actor-singer has mastered that journey without recourse to false behavior, there is no reason to execute it each time he gets up to sing. All performances of his material will now begin with Exercise 2, where each of us takes up residence in our dreams: Center stage. Mr. M.'s moves downstage are more controlled and DC suggests he continue on through the Verse and into the second "8" of the Chorus. He is stopped at the Bridge. DC congratulates him and explains that, because the mechanics of the steps stay the same, there is no need to sing through to the Rideout. Mr. M. has demonstrated that he not only understands the nature of the work but, more to the point, has experienced the physical sensation of matching the move to the measure of each "fill." Asked to describe this:

MR. M.

As I moved down, I felt as though the air around me was resisting me. It was like ... like moving through black jello. (A reference to the blackout and the front lighting in the studio.)

DC
(To Mr. M)

I like that. The idea of resistance from the theater presages, in its way, the relationship between the performer and his audience. Never presume that because you are singing you have the attention of the listener. I don't even suggest you ask for it. Demand it. (See Chapter Seventeen: The Performance.)

Her Work—The Leading Lady

Miss H. is at that age when life—as well as prevarication—is said to begin. Unlike others for whom those years can bring on the doldrums, her toothsome smile is not only exhausting but possibly counterfeit. DC, unwilling to make too drastic a change, chooses Irving Berlin's rueful "Fools Fall in Love":

VERSE	Why do I allow my heart	
	To make decisions for me?	
	Why do I keep lis'tning to my heart?	(*Air*)
	Why do I get so involved	
	When I would rather be free?	
	Maybe it's because I'm not so smart:	(*Air*)
1ST "8"	Fools fall in love	
(A)	Only lunatics fall in love	
	And I'm a fool	(*Air*)

2ND "8"	Fools seek romance	
(A)	Only idiots take a chance	
	And I'm a fool	*(Air)*
BRIDGE	I should be able to put all my feelings aside	
(B)	I would be able to take one free ride	
	...in my stride	*(Air)*
LAST "8"	But fools cannot play	
(A)	They get serious right away	
	And break the rule	*(Air)*
	My heart's on fire	
	When I know I ought to keep cool	*(Air)*
	Fools fall in love	
	And I'm such a fool.	

("Fools Fall in Love," words and music by Irving Berlin, from *Louisiana Purchase*, 1940. Copyright © 1940 by Irving Berlin. Copyright renewed by Irving Berlin. Reprinted by permission of Irving Berlin Music Corporation.)

Miss H. accepts DC's choice of "wrong song" with her customary ebullience. It seems that even its plaintive air of self-recrimination may be done in by her relentless high spirits. Like the others before her, she retires into the wings to prepare for her entrance.

Irving Berlin, one of America's greatest and most prolific masters, died in 1989, more than a century old. About him Alec Wilder, in his *American Popular Song: The Great Innovators 1900-1950* (New York: Oxford University Press, 1972) has written: "Admirers of the music of Jerome Kern, Richard Rodgers and Cole Porter are, in my experience, unlikely to consider Berlin's work in the same category. I believe that out of forgetfulness and confusion, they are inclined to minimize his talents." His music and lyrics (like Porter, he never worked with anyone other than himself) have a deceptive air of modesty—but there is more to them than meets the ear. The Verse of "Fools Fall in Love" is in ad lib and the Chorus AABA, as marked. Of particular interest:

1. The "A" theme, although referred to by its generic name "8," is only six bars long.

2. The Bridge, "B," is the standard eight bars in length, but the last "8" is fourteen bars long.

3. The last word of the first "8," " ... fool," is scored on the third of the key, A, in which the song is written (F Major). When the same word ends the second "8," it rises, with consequent dramatic effect, to the fifth of the key-C. In the last "8," the same theme recurs on the line " ... And break the rule," but now the word " ... rule" climbs higher to the

sixth of the key-D—to achieve even more drama as it swells into the final bars of music on the lyric " ... My heart's on fire, etc. ... "

Here, the perfect example of Berlin's genius—a composer whose songs never mistake the simplistic for the truly simple.

Miss H. enters. DC is determined to deal with all that unbridled good humor. Miss H. is confused. It seems no one has ever criticized her natural vivacity.

DC
(To Miss H. and the Class)

To say that one behaves naturally does not imply, under the circumstances of this exercise, that your behavior is necessarily correct or good. I have asked each of you to make an entrance and dare to leave yourself alone. We all know now how difficult this is to do. It is my task, like the mirror in *Snow White*, to tell you what I see as objectively and as honestly as I can. A mirror is a reflection, not an adversary. (See Chapter Five: "A Game: The You Nobody Knows.") At an audition, you not only *want* to know how you are seen by those who are auditioning you, you *must* know. Only then will you be able to edit your work. There is no need to be likable, to be charming, to be angry, to be haughty, to be humble, to be defensive, to be anything but who you are. Again, remember, your work is being judged from the moment you come into sight. Do not make the error of thinking that your audition begins with a song. It begins with you.

Miss H., after many tries, begins to risk showing her realer self. DC applauds her effort to let go and suggests that she continue to work on the problem when she rehearses at home. She moves upstage and goes on with the exercise. He stops her at the completion of the first downstage step.

DC
(To Miss H.)

The beginning of the step is well timed. But it came to an end too soon when you made your base on the downbeat of the first word of the new line. Let me show you. (*DC joins her on stage. They sing together:*)

Why do I allow my heart to make decisions for me?
Why do I keep list'ning to my heart?   *(Air)*

⌐ Why do I get so involved
    When I would rather be free?

(*He makes his base incorrectly, with her, on the downbeat of the third "Why ... " Continuing to both Miss H. and the Class*) It is important to keep the arc of "Air" alive by resisting the urge to end its life as soon as you hear yourself begin to sing. Keep the step alive well into the middle of the new line. A good picture to keep in mind: Just like the roof of a house, the "Air" extends to, and overhangs farther than, the vertical walls in order to make the eaves. The step begins at the *start* of the last word of the line but it finishes *beyond* the beginning of the new line. (*DC moves upstage to demonstrate. This time his base comes to its final rest around the words " ... get so involved ... "*)

Why do I allow my heart to make decisions for me?
<u>Why do I keep list'ning to my heart?</u>   (*Air*)
Why do I get so involved
    When I would rather be free?

(*Miss H. tries it alone with increasing skill as she sings further into the song. DC praises her and sums up Exercise 3 for her and the Class.*) It is at this point that the actor-singer should begin to see that there is a concept at work here in direct opposition to what he has heretofore been accustomed to. Until today, when you picked up a piece of music, you saw a "sung" phrase followed by a musical fill. It looked like this:

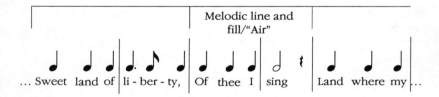

The "fill" or "Air" on the word " ... sing" seems to belong to the line you *have been* singing—a musical finish, so to speak, that rounds out the line. The purpose of Exercise 3 is to introduce you to a new and, for the actor, intriguing revelation: The "Air" rather than filling the *last* moments of what you have sung is, in fact, the music that introduces what you are *going to* sing. It is in this "Air" that you will create the *implicit* cue that will birth the next sung line. Again, using "My Country 'Tis of Thee" as the illustration, the above marking will now be seen as:

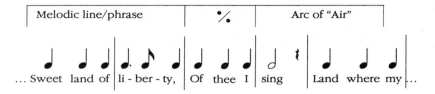

Exercise 3 is designed to educate the actor-singer to recognize and deal with the specific length of each musical space within the body of the song to be sung. Inevitably, the steps that time these "Air" pockets will be replaced with acting beats. For now, we are restrained from acting the song before we know the difference between what we are singing and what we are singing about. The nature of all text (in this case, the lyric) is that it is the child of subtext. We do not speak mindlessly; we must not sing mindlessly. These are unchallengeable facts. But before you choose the inner cues that will give the appearance of life to what you sing, you must be made aware of the mathematical precision that defines all music. Only then, when the form and shape of music is inherent in your thinking, will you be able to give content a place in which to live.

Exercise 4, in Chapter Nine, returns to the primary impulse that motivates all speech, whether it is spoken or sung: focus. The *what* you sing will always take second position to the *to whom* you are singing it.

9

Focus

All I see is my reflected eye.

—Elder Olson

EXERCISE 4: SPOTTING

Until now we have been singing to one focus: Center. But there is an infinity of "spots" into which you may play: high, low, higher, lower, left, right, and, in an ever-widening lateral shift, to the left of left and to the right of right. Short of singing into the wings, you may sing, generally, to anywhere and, specifically, to anyone you choose. However, a technique that swings from the restriction of unifocus (Center) to the permissiveness of infinity would have little value. As a way station between these extremes, Exercise 4 focuses on three spots: Center (C), the most commanding of attention, and Left (L) and Right (R) of Center. It is imperative, however, that the reader remember that we are now speaking only of the *technique of spotting*. When you are *performing* a song—which is quite another matter—focusing solely to C, L, and R would be too arbitrary and confining. Furthermore, we are still concerned with learning a technique. As a means to an end, it will be visible at all times. Later, technique will become the substructure that supports your performance. It will then be seen by an audience only when it is improperly executed.

All songs should begin C. This rule applies to both the practice of technique and the performance of sung material. When you are performing, that Center focus need not linger there—in fact, if the song is meant to be sung to the entire theater, it may stay C for just a moment or two before your focus "travels," but any song that starts to an arbitrary L or R for no reason other than " ... I happened to be looking there when it was time to sing" incurs a corresponding reaction: " ... Why is he singing to the side of the house?" Spotting Center will always give importance to the words you are about to sing, and the importance of the words you sing, in the order of their importance, is:

1. the first line of the Verse;
2. the last line of the Verse (if possible);
3. the first line of the Chorus;
4. the first line of the Bridge, or Release;
5. the last line of the Chorus.

By choosing to sing the above-listed five lines of your song to a Center focus, you now know that the line that precedes each one of those lines may be played to a lateral focus. This occurred once before when, in Exercise 2, you came C at the top of the third bar of the Vamp from either L or R of C (depending upon the direction toward which you turned when you nodded to your pianist).

As you fill in your focus choices, remember that it is not significant whether you go R or L on a line that is "spotted" to the lateral, but I do suggest that the line following it, at least when technique is all you have on your mind, be played to the Center spot. This will guard against playing L, R, L, R, L, R, etc. and risking a horizontal yo-yo effect that, from out front, gives the impression that you are watching a tennis match. It is not mere whim that compels the beginner to work anywhere but straight front. Too often he evades coping with a Center focus because, unconsciously, he feels its inherent power. Naked fear repels him from the big C, for it would be tantamount to looking the audience straight in the eye. Unsure of the tactics to use, he is unwilling to take command. The shifting, shifty spotting advertises not so much his unwillingness to sing as his ignorance of how and to whom to do it. After all, the novice may be coaxed into singing, especially if he needs the job, but he cannot be expected to do it well for the same reason.

Guided by the above plan, work your way through the lyric, electing which lines of the lyric will be "spotted" Center, Left, and Right, and then mark your choices in the sheet-music copy of your song. The final plotting should, within the allowable margins of probability, look like this: C—L (or R)—C—R (or L)—C—L (or R)—C—R (or L), etc.

Unlike the steps we have been taking to define the "Air" in the song, spot changes have nothing to do with the music of a song and all to do with its lyric. The rule: Change focus when you have finished what you were saying to one "spot" and have something further to say (sing) to another part of the theater or the room. In Exercise 4, practice "spotting" whenever you can, remembering that the sequence will always remain the same: "spot" and then sing.

Whenever a focus change occurs on a line on which you plan to "do" something (by "do something" I mean a physical act as set apart from standing at zero, including, for example, a gesture or a walk), the spot change must *precede* that physical act. The only *doing* we have been concerned with up until now is the step downstage that physicalizes "Air," so if there is an opportunity to change focus and a musical "fill" separates the two lines, *be sure your spot change precedes the step you have been taking.* In other words, when a focus change happens to accompany a line on which you plan to move—spot, move, and then sing.

When you work the technique in Exercise 4, the sequence will always be:

First, you have someone to sing to (spot), and then you have something to say (sing).

In the performance of a song, the sequence will change to:

First, you have someone to sing to (spot) and then, if there is something you want to do (move), and then speak (sing).

Don'ts

1. Never change focus in the middle of a sentence. Finish what you went there to say and *then* relate to the new "spot." This is not only good manners but sane behavior.

2. When you work to a lateral spot, be sure you do not go too far to the L or R. Just as Center focus is inclined to go too high, lateral focus tends to go too wide. If you think of yourself as the aperture of a camera eye, you are at the point where those "spots" converge. In the reverse, as they leave you, they move away from each other to distances much farther apart than you can possibly be aware of until this is brought to your attention. Incorrect:

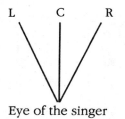

Eye of the singer

The corrected narrowing of the lateral spots:

Eye of the singer

As you can see, a minimum switch from C to L or R creates a line that moves farther and farther away from Center. When in doubt about how wide is too wide, take a step to the left or right, focus straight ahead of you, then leave your eyes there and return your feet to the old Center position. You are now spotting to a lateral focus no wider than it needs to be. To those out front who are watching you work, too wide a spot will give the illusion that you are playing to the side wall. Worse, you will be unaware that you are ignoring the entire house. If this were to occur on a punch line, you would lose your laugh simply because the theater would not have seen/heard the joke.

3. Don't wait to change focus until the last word is dead on your lips. As soon as it begins, spot L, R, or C. You will still be singing the word but—go! On time is, of course, perfect. A little early—not so bad. Late—inexcusable. In fact, the old saw: "Better late than never" does not apply to singing. Change it to: "When you are late, don't leave at all."

Do's

1. Try as many focus changes as the song permits. This is an exercise in technique. Whether you would choose that many changes in a

performance of the song is not germane now.

2. If the song is objective ("you" appears throughout the lyric) or subjective ("I" and/or "me" is the recurring pronoun), practice focus changes regardless of their relevancy. If you were singing a *house number* (a lyric meant for everyone in the room or in the theater), the single Center spot would have felt restrictive. Now you will be liberated, at least to the degree that, in Exercise 4, you are singing to the Center and to the Left and Right. Conversely, if you had been singing a love song, the exclusivity of the Center focus would have supported the intimacy of the lyric. Now, with three spots to play to, you will be pouring out your feelings to three lovers, rather than to one. Put logic aside for now. You are practicing spot changes. What is important is that you cannot perfect the technique without a song.

3. Should you freeze your focus choices? For now, yes. When you are performing, however, I do not suggest a frozen spot plan. But at that point in your work, you will always know where you must be at significant lines in the lyric: Center.

ONE-SIDED DIALOGUE

The Ingenue

Miss R. is archetypal. Like the character actor, a wrong song can only be expected to help age the young lady. Whereas most actor-singers resist the wrong song (they are only too aware that DC is making a camouflaged but, nevertheless, editorial comment on them), the ingenue and the juvenile embrace it. It is probable evidence of their discomfort with the insipidity of the roles relegated to them by virtue of their youth. Miss R. is only too happy to have assigned to her George and Ira Gershwin's "Boy! What Love Has Done to Me!"

The placement of the focus changes as indicated below may strike the reader as eccentric until it becomes clear that each change is placed above *the last word of a line* so that the new line inherits the change in good time. The goal, here, is to prevent a change of focus from occurring so late that it arrives right on the down beat of the new line.

Center (C) focus on the third bar of the Vamp

1ST "8"   I fetch his slippers
(A)   (L) →
           Fill up the pipe he smokes
           I cook the kippers

(C) →
Laugh at his oldest jokes
Yet here I anchor
(stay C for the title)
I might have had a banker
(R) →
Boy! What love has done to me! (*Air*)
2ND "8" My life he's wrecking
(A)   *(stay R to finish the sentence)*
Bet you could find him now
Out somewhere necking
(C) →
Somebody else's frau!
You get to know life
(L) *(no need to center title after the 1st "8")*
When married to a low-life
(C) *(for the Bridge)*
Boy! What love has done to me! (*Air*)
BRIDGE I can't hold my head up
(B)   The butcher, the baker,
All know he's a faker
Brother, I am fed up!
(L) →
But if I left him I'd be all at sea (*Air*)
LAST "8" I'm just a slavey
(A)   Life is a funny thing
(C) →
He's got the gravy
(R) →
I got a wedding ring
(C) →
But I have grown so
(stay C for last line)
I love the dirty so 'n so!
Boy! What love has done to me!

("Boy! What Love Has Done to Me," music and lyrics by George and Ira
Gershwin, from *Girl Crazy*, 1930. Copyright © 1930 New World Music Corp.
Copyright renewed. All rights reserved. Used by permission.)

The lateral spot change on " … I have grown so" must return to a
Center spot for " … I love the dirty so 'n so" because this is the power
line in the lyric. The spot remains Center for the last line because the
revelation is so stunning following, as it does, the long derogatory list
of the lady's unhappiness with the man. Not only her surprise in the
confession of her love for him (she could not have known she would

say that when she first began the song) but the witty rhyme she chooses in which to say it seemed to me to demand the intensity that remaining in Center affords.

Miss R., like the others before her, is in the wings preparing to enter.

DC
(*To the Class*)

"Boy! What Love Has Done to Me!" is from the George and Ira Gershwin score for *Girl Crazy*, produced in 1930. The show is of historic significance in that it introduced, for the first time on any stage, Ginger Rogers and Ethel Merman. Miss Merman sang the song under discussion, as well as the unforgettable "I Got Rhythm" and "Sam and Delilah." When you add "Embraceable You," "Bidin' My Time," "Treat Me Rough," "Could You Use Me?" and the lovely "But Not for Me," there is more than enough evidence to support the claim of a large body of musical theater experts who consider the score the finest of all Gershwin's work, excepting his masterpiece: *Porgy and Bess*. Song for song, no other Gershwin score contains as many "standard" hits. Adding further weight to the piece's distinction: The pit orchestra, led by Red Nichols, included among its personnel Benny Goodman, Gene Krupa, Glen Miller, Jack Teagarden, and Jimmy Dorsey!

As for "Boy! What Love Has Done to Me!" I have omitted the published Verse for reasons of length, and combined the lyrics from the two published Choruses in order to gain the best of each. Although both lyrics have enough value to stand on their own, two Choruses at an audition do not guarantee double enjoyment. The old show-business saw, "leave them wanting more," is still good advice.

The song, as marked, is AABA. The Bridge is not easy to sing. There are octave jumps on " ... head up" and " ... fed up," and syncopated quasiinstrumental musical phrases that require a certain fluency with jazz. However, as in the case of all Gershwin songs (again, with the exception of arias from *Porgy and Bess*), the performer can cheat around vocal corners without doing any great damage to the tune. Unlike the work of Jerome Kern, whose melodies generally require a certain vocal splendor, Gershwin is better served by a stylish, more swinging presentation. Performers, as a group, do him greater service than the straight out-and-out singer. For substantiation, one need only research who first introduced his songs. Among them: Fred Astaire, Gertrude Lawrence, Gaxton and Moore, Clifton Webb, John W. Bubbles, and Avon Long (both historic Sportin' Life's), Gracie Allen and George

Burns, Ginger Rogers, and Jack Buchanan. This is not to say that singers should deprive themselves of the particular joy of singing a Gershwin song. Streisand, Horne, Garland, Fitzgerald, Vaughan, McCrae, Bennett, Sinatra, Tormé, Damone, and, to a lesser extent (although with greater "sound"), Te Kanawa, Farrell, Domingo—all have recorded him with results that range from perfect to pedestrian.

Miss R.'s entrance and Vamp have been commented on during a previous Class session. DC is eager to see her performance of the "Air" in the Gershwin song and her mastery of the technique of focus changes. (These have been marked in the lyric as printed above.) She sings through the first two "8s" and the first half of the Bridge before DC interrupts:

DC

(To Miss R.)

In your eagerness to move when the "Air" begins—as practiced correctly in Exercise 3—you are moving too soon, before the spot change has been executed. You must understand that the step will be replaced with an acting beat that is related to what you are going to say (sing). Don't be guilty of telegraphing that until you have committed yourself to the new "to whom" you are going to say it to, namely: the new "spot." The adjustment belongs to "it." Now, let's pick it up on the title line, played Center, that ends the first "8" and continue into the first line of the second "8," directed to the Right.

Miss R. attempts the spot change and the step downstage that fills the "Air" between the first two "8s" but, again, the work is not cleanly performed.

DC

Try to change the spot and cut the move downstage. Perhaps then you will be able to distinguish between what are two distinct and separate acts.

Miss R. again sings the title line that ends the first "8" and on the word " ... me" makes a narrow focus change to the R. But this time, she does not move downstage. DC asks her to repeat the technique until it is perfectly timed.

DC

Now, out of the context of the rhythm of the song, let's try the line again, and when you have changed focus from C to R, and only then, shift your weight and move downstage.

DC instructs the pianist to go out of tempo on the downbeat of the last word of the line, " ... me," in order to allow Miss R. time to spot and move without the demands of rhythm. Miss R. now sings the line to C, spots R on the "m" of " ... me" and then, indulging in the permissiveness of a rhythmless "fill," waits a moment, and shifts her weight and moves downstage, spotting narrowly to the R throughout the life of the step. After consolidating this sequence by repetition, DC speaks.

DC

Well done. Of course, now you will have to do it within the strict rhythm of Gershwin's musical "fill." Again, as you refine the technique, always keep in mind to whom are you *now* singing (spot change) and then begin your follow-through with the step that sets up the new line, in this case " ... My life he's wrecking." Of great importance is the timing of when that spot change occurs. Too soon, from out front, would look like you were singing " ... Boy, what love has done to" and then switched to the R for " ... me." The trick is to be eager to "get on with it" without getting on with it by failing to finish what you had to say. That R focus must not be born until C has received its full due—the complete line.

The following steps in the techniques we have been working to perfect have been covered in Exercises 1 through 4:

1. the Entrance;
2. the time spent in Center stage before the actual song begins;
3. the nod to the accompanist;
4. the performance of the Vamp;
5. the steps downstage that delimit the time span of the musical "fills" or "Air";
6. the execution of three arbitrary spots—C, L, and R—out of the infinity of choices of focus to which you may work.

These six drills, performed in four exercises, complete the first half of the technical work that takes place in the Classes I teach. Chapters Ten through Fifteen are concerned with techniques that are of equal importance but exclusive of the work we have already covered.

SOME OBSERVATIONS

When the Wrong Song Seems Right—and Why

It is not difficult for me to choose the wrong song at the beginning of a Class for, after all, the actor-singer is a stranger to me and, as in all classes, the members are unknown to each other. Even when an actor of repute sits in the Class, the persona of his public image is vastly different from what the class and I see. However, as the weeks elapse, the chemistry in the room undergoes marked changes, subtle in the beginning but increasingly obvious as the time goes by. Outlanders become insiders and even foes turn into friends as the class seems to seek its personal profile. It is always a point of fascination to me that a group, chosen out of the happenstance of who called when and so formless when it first convenes, metamorphoses into a single body with a distinct personality.

Chief among the surprises this conversion creates concerns the "wrong songs" that the class and I unanimously agreed upon when they were first assigned to the members of the group. There, before our eyes—by the end of the session—what was once ill-chosen seems now to be material expressly written for them. Does this nullify my original choice of song? Not at all. But we should all know that, when we sing songs that show the recessive side of ourselves, the combination of what is *heard* with what is dominant and, therefore, *seen,* presents the real and the *true* us. Unfortunately, casting in the musical theater is categorical. Those who cast the show, destined as they are never to know the real and true us, see us through the eyes of a stranger. At an audition, the "wrong song" (although it may present us in the rounded way we are perceived—blindly and with forgiveness—by our friends, lovers, husbands, and wives) does us a disservice. The "right song" is the one that presents you as you *appear* to be. The songs you choose to sing must never be allowed to confuse the auditioner. What he hears must corroborate what he sees. Yes, you must always sing what is fitting to the circumstances: the ingenue, an ingenue song; the juvenile, a juvenile song; the character man or woman, a pertinent character song—songs that correspond to the roles called for on the casting sheet that you, by all appearances, can be expected to play. However, *what you are thinking while you sing that song is for you to choose.* It is there, in your *unheard* song, that the wrong song will be indirectly but visibly sung.

IS DOING NOTHING SOMETHING?

I am often told by a student whom I have taught for a short period of time that he gained employment in a musical by "doing nothing" at his audition. Not having been with me long enough to learn how to *perform* anything, he elected to sing the only song he knew—the one he had worked on in the First Technique Class. I assume he stood still (the downstage steps were cut to avoid confusion), spotted C, L, and R, and risked nothing else. Since the reach of most auditions far exceeds the performer's grasp, Jean-Paul Richter's remark that "a variety of nothing is better than a monotony of something" was corroborated. But even Herr Richter would not argue that, when a richer physical statement would work to the benefit of a performance, a good something is indisputably better than a good nothing. The technical work in the following chapters explores that "good something."

We have been concerned with:
1. the physical language placed on a song held down to "zero;"
2. learning how to time the musical "Air" that fills the spaces between the lines we sing;
3. the importance of a sane focus through the fourth wall.

For the present, these techniques will be put aside as we move on to the subject of *body language*—its hows, whys, wheres, and, most particularly, its whens.

10

Introduction to Five Technical Exercises on a Lyric

Don't just stand there, do something.
—Corrected version of an intramural show-biz
admonition

It would never occur to an actor, during the rehearsal period of a play, to ask his director, "What do I do with my hands?" and yet it is a question that nags and distresses him from the beginning of his study of the art of singing on stage. The born singer-cum-performer is spared this physical self-consciousness. The wellspring of his talent, being natural, somehow induces a totality of vocal and physical expression that spares him this agony. I distinguish between the actor, the actor-singer, and the singer who can perform, for the purpose of identification rather than debate. John Gielgud, Laurence Olivier, Marlon Brando, and Dustin Hoffman are actors; the late Robert Preston (*The Music Man*), Rex Harrison (*My Fair Lady*), and Angela Lansbury (in *Mame* and *Sweeney Todd*) are actor-singers; Frank Sinatra, Barbra Streisand, and Lena Horne are singer-performers. Crossovers can, and often do, blur the lines of distinction. The late Judy Garland and today's Bernadette

Peters, Joel Grey, and, again, Miss Streisand live comfortably in all three groups while many singers, both serious and "pop," can act within a competency range that stretches from extraordinary (the late Maria Callas) to first-rate (the French Yves Montand) down to .... Without recourse to name-calling, it is even possible, in the case of the singer-performer, to hair-split the hyphenate to favor one or the other half of the classification. There are singers who cannot be considered performers because, apart from the quality of voice, their work is too simplistic to hold an audience, while conversely, there are performers whose charm and power of personality preempts any harsh criticism of their singing.

For the neophyte, singing on stage can take on all the appearances of a neurosis by seeming to release a veritable Pandora's box of hangups. Throats close, jaws tighten, tongues swell, shoulders lift, breath comes in short pants, arms stiffen—all because he is committing a natural act that, like dancing, man has been doing since the dawn of time. This is not to say that some of us are not more blessed than others in our ability to sing or dance, but there is considerable comfort in the knowledge that no adjudicated law forbids us to raise whatever voice we do have in song, or to move around a dance floor to the sound of music.

Physical problems are not the only tormenters. "Indicating" and "playing the words" are breaches of know-how an actor would not be guilty of or tolerate in others, yet will commit without conscience when he first begins to sing. Unhappily, these crimes are more grievous in singing than they are in acting. Although it advertises the absence of craft and the banality of the amateur's thinking, bad acting can go unnoticed by audiences and critics alike. But the least discerning eye and musical ear can identify the amateur singer. Further, whereas a bad actor may never know his shortcomings, the beginner actor-singer is all too aware of his inadequacies. The pain of hearing himself sing and the empty gestures and meaningless charades he appliqués onto the songs he sings irritate his personal aesthetic. The dilemma rankles: How does he rid himself of the physical self-consciousness.

Body language is the result of a shadowy kaleidoscope of thought impulses that feed what we are thinking into our motor system. It may duplicate what we say or move in a counterpoint more complicated and revealing than the words we speak. We are all, to some extent, prisoners of the limitations of our vocabularies, but each of us is a Bernard Shaw in our ability to invent the rich variety of subtextual movement that decorates *what* we say with the physical language that proclaims what we *mean* by what we say.

When speech is deprived of this second track, a bizarre inversion occurs. Instead of the singer singing the song, *the song appears to be singing him.* With nothing on his mind but the lyric he is singing, the range of gesture is limited to: hands up and down, hands out, in and down once more, one hand up and down, the other hand up and down again—or an indication of what is being said (sung), e.g., pointing out pronouns like "you" and "me." This is not a heinous crime. There are too many actors, singers, actor-singers, and performers who are guilty of it. But when all you do is sing a song in this monophonic fashion, you run the risk that someone may sing it better than you do.

It is our unique humanness that gives our work its individuality. With only the song on our mind, that singularity is diminished. At the moment when the actor-singer acknowledges this, he takes the first steps toward answering the nagging and distressing question: "What do I do with my hands?"

At the top of Chapter Eight, I named the three "how-to's" that comprise the techniques to be learned in the study of "Air":
1. how to identify it;
2. how to time it;
3. how to fill it.

Chapter Two, identified it. Chapter Eight, timed it. Now, in Chapter Eleven, we are ready to replace the downstage steps that defined the length of the musical "fill" with our own creative thought processes. If, as described above, physical self-consciousness is the direct result of having only the lyric of the song on your mind, it is time to create the unheard script for the eye to see—the one that explicates the lyric that the ear hears.

The following five chapters concentrate on the physicalization of subtext and its application to singing. As in the case of all that has gone before, *it is a technique* to be worked on a song and *not a performance of the song.* Chapters Eleven, Twelve, and Thirteen do not require an accompanist. Hallelujah!

11

The "One"

And bad thinking do not wrest true speaking.
—William Shakespeare

No music accompanies the next three chapters. Its absence will help you to see and to understand the words as *script*. Remember: We are still mastering a technique to be performed on a song. At no time should you allow yourself to think that it is the song you are performing.

THE "ONE"

The "One" is the first of five exercises derived from and superimposed on an assigned lyric. Its object: to tell, as objectively as you can, and *in your own words*, the tale told by the lyric. Perhaps because you have not taken the time, in the past, to read a lyric in your eagerness to sing its song, it will come as something of a surprise to discover how much detail a good lyric offers you. The intention of the "One" is to isolate all the information, both of story and of character, that can be read *in* a lyric without reading anything *into* it—a deceptively simple task. The difficulty lies in maintaining strict objectivity. No "I think" or "I would say ..." and no moral judgements—just the facts.

117

Further:

1. Begin the "One" with the sentence: "This is a story about ..." Is it a man? A woman? A boy? A girl? May either gender speak the lyric? Who, then, is narrating the tale? Begin the "One" with "This is a story about a man ...," "...a woman," or, if it is so, "...a story about a man or a woman," "... a boy or a girl." (An interesting revelation: many songs may not be denied you for the reason of gender although custom may have made it seem otherwise. Songs relegated to women may, upon careful reading of the lyric, be equally valid when they are sung by a man, with the reverse equally true.)

2. Where does the lyric take place? If there is a place named, so much the better—e.g., Porter's "I Happen to Like New York," Rodgers and Hart's "Manhattan," Gershwin's "A Foggy Day (... in London Town)," Webber and Rice's "Don't Cry for Me, Argentina." When the location is not named, tell me, as objectively as you can, whether the setting is urban, rural, suburban, or even exurban, if that "far out" is defensible.

3. In what general economic bracket can the narrator of the tale be placed? You may use this gauge: lower-lower, middle-lower, upper-lower, lower-middle, middle-middle, upper-middle, lower-upper, middle-upper, and upper-upper class, or a range that may include a combination of more than one. If there is not sufficient information, permit yourself an educated guess. For example: Rodgers and Hart's "Manhattan" is sung by either a young man or a young woman who can be found somewhere between the middle-lower and upper-middle classes. Why? He or she—the lyric can be sung by either sex—has an apartment in Manhattan ("I've a cozy little flat in what is known as old Manhattan") or in Flatbush (depending on which chorus you choose to sing), and, as stated in the lyric, he uses the subway to get around town. These brackets are inferential guesses but, in New York, paying rent for an apartment, no matter how small, excludes you from the lower-lower-class category and the need to get around town by subway and bus would tend to rule out a member of the upper class for whom the cost of owning a car or taking a taxi whenever one cares to would not be prohibitive.

4. How much schooling has the narrator had? Here, too, you will rarely find the information stated, but choice of language, style of speech, and quality of insight will offer significant clues.

5. Finally, what is the narrator's approximate age? Again, through objective inference, set it in three categories: the *maximal* age (thirties, forties, fifties—all the way up to the nineties if nothing in the lyric forbids it); the *minimal* age (teens, early 20s); the *optimal* age (the age that best serves the intentions of the writer). Do not name a specific number: twenty-three, twenty-four, twenty-five, twenty-six, and twenty-seven are more correctly referred to as mid-twenties. When you are unable to be even that general, an allowable answer would be: anywhere from late twenties to mid-thirties, or anywhere from low forties to upper fifties.

To help you to keep an objective distance, remember:

    1. Use your own language. Don't quote from the lyric.

    2. Resist personal assessments or moral judgements of either the narrator or the event being narrated. Cut out "I's" and "Me's" from the "One." "... I would say that," "... I do (or don't) think that etc." are verboten.

    3. A suggestion: Think of the exercise as reportage and be ready to defend the facts if challenged. Your defense will lie only in those facts and not in what you assumed the lyric said.

Why a "One?" By separating the words from the music assigned to them, you will be freed from making performance choices that are evoked by knee-jerk emotional responses to the music: a sad song sung sadly, a pretty ballad sung prettily, a blues sung in a blue spotlight. Of the five exercises in this section, only a "One," were you to work it on all the songs you sing, would be to your advantage. You cannot know what a lyric means (the cornerstone of all performances) until you know for certain what it says.

DIALOGUES

Her Work

Miss W. is a young actress of exceeding range who is not permitted to vent her sense of humor on anything blither than television's police melodramas. To lighten her professional load, DC assigns a script of Cole Porter's:

VERSE   Since I went on the wagon, I'm
              Certain drink is a major crime
              For, when you lay off the liquor
              You feel so much slicker,
              Well, that is most of the time.
              But there are moments, sooner or later,

When it's tough, I've got to say,
Not to say, "Waiter,"
1ST "8"   Make it another Old-Fashioned, please
(A)   Make it another double Old-Fashioned, please.
2ND "8"   Make it for one who's due
(B)   To join the disillusioned crew
Make it for one of love's new refugees.
3RD "8"   Once, high in my castle, I reigned supreme
(A)   And oh! What a castle,
Built on a heavenly dream!
LAST "8"   Then, quick as a light'ning flash
(B)   That castle began to crash!
So make it another Old-Fashioned, please!
CODA   Leave out the cherry
Leave out the orange
Leave out the bitters,
Just make it a straight rye.

Miss W. is ready. Since stage demeanor is not relevant to the performance of a "One," she brings a chair from the wings to center stage and sits. Before she begins, DC supplies background intelligence.

DC
(To Miss W. and the Class)

"Make It Another Old-Fashioned, Please," written by Cole Porter in 1940, is from *Panama Hattie,* followed by the scores for the film *You'll Never Get Rich* in 1941, and, in the same year, the Broadway shows *Let's Face It, Something for the Boys* in 1943, the film *Mississippi Belle* in 1943–44, and again on Broadway, *Mexican Hayride* in 1944, and, in the same year, *Seven Lively Arts,* and *Around the World in Eighty Days* in 1946, and, finally, for the screen in 1948, *The Pirate. Panama Hattie* began what has been referred to as Porter's dry years. Coupled with great physical pain incurred from injuries and subsequent surgeries sustained after a fall from a horse in 1937, he was further burdened by a whispering campaign that implied his career was over. This burned-out has-been was still to write his magnum opus, *Kiss Me Kate* and the scores for *Out of This World, Can-Can, Silk Stockings,* and, for the screen, *High Society* and *Les Girls,* and, lastly, for television, *Aladdin*—any one of which possesses, at the very least, one "standard" hit. The song assigned to Miss W., with its intricate rhyme structure in the Verse, is prime Porter, and the luscious melody of the Chorus has a bittersweet joke in the Coda as an added lagniappe. *(To Miss W.)* I think we may begin now, but I will be interrupting you by acting as an interlocutor for the Class. They do not know the lyric and you and I are both determined that they receive the "One" as uneditorialized fact. When I take exception to something you say it is motivated only toward that end.

MISS W.

This is a story about a woman who ...

DC

Is there anything in the lyric that would prevent a man from singing this song?

MISS W.

Well, I think ...

DC

I?

MISS W.

Sorry about that. *(She rechecks the lyric.)* I would've sworn that only a woman could sing this script.

DC

In a way, you were correct. A man would not be prohibited from singing it, but in a "One" you might add that the tone of the language tips the scale toward the probability that a woman is the narrator of the story ...

Once, high in my castle, I reigned supreme
And oh! What a castle!
Built on a heavenly dream!

121

These are words that only a man who is an ex-king could speak without some discomfort, whereas an audience would not think they were lines from a tale told by an ex-queen. In actual fact, the song was sung, in its original context, by Ethel Merman.

MISS W.

Well then. This is a story about a man or a woman, more probably a woman, whose minimal age I would say ... oops, sorry ... cut that ...

DC

Good.

MISS W.

She is minimally eighteen or twenty-one, depending on what state of the Union we find her in.

DC

Why do you say that?

MISS W.

Because she is in a bar drinking hard liquor.

DC

Very good. Do we know what particular drink she favors?

MISS W.

Yes. Rye Old-Fashioneds.

DC

How old dare she be?

MISS W.

Late forties or early fifties.

DC

Do you mean to say that she may not sing this song if she is in her late fifties?

MISS W.

Well, perhaps.

DC

How about her sixties? Or even her seventies?

MISS W.

That would be stretching it.

DC

The lady tells us that the man with whom she was living suddenly up and left her. By the way, were they married?

MISS W.

She doesn't say.

DC

Arguable though it may be, I can't see why, at any age, this experience would be denied her.

MISS W.

It wasn't denied my mother. (*The Class reacts.*)

DC

(*Unwilling to pursue that subject*) Well then, you agree that the desertion gains dramatic poignancy if they had been together for a long, rather than a short, time? By the way, could death have been the cause of his sudden absence?

MISS W.

You know, that crossed my mind. The fact is that there is no actual mention of why or under what circumstances he left her. But somehow death seemed so far from the quality of her grief that I put it aside.

DC

I tend to agree with you. The word never appears but nothing, again in a "One," should be left uninvestigated. His death is a possibility if not a probability. To return to her age, you do agree that the desertion gains poignancy if they were together a long, rather than a short, time?

MISS W.

Oh yes. As a matter of fact, I knew, right from the start, she was not going to be too young. As you say, it can happen to anyone at any time but if her age is way down there, you just don't care. She may be in pain when a love affair or a marriage comes to an end, but at that age, there's plenty of time for healing to take place. Not to mention the probability that there will be a replacement in her future.

DC

First-rate. What did you choose for her optimal age?

MISS W.

Somewhere in her forties. Not so old as to break your heart and not so young that you don't care one way or the other. There's another clue in the lyric for her being older rather than younger and that's her choice of drink. It's a drink with a perfect name. It wasn't even in my dictionary. Only when I asked a friend who doubles as a bartender did I find out what kind of cocktail it is. How do you suggest the actor handle this?

DC

The lyric speaks of old-fashioneds but the script has nothing to do with liquor. Here is a perfect example of the two elements with which we will be working: the verbal content—what the words *say*—and their significance—the *subtext* that is the "Two" (the exercise that follows). Macbeth's wassail cup was filled with spiced ale, Falstaff drank his burnt sack, and Stephano and Trinculo are drunk on grog, but they are no less playable today because their tastes don't run to straight-up martinis, Bloody Marys, and vodka sours. When the curtain rises, is it more important for us to hear whether the lady has fallen off the wagon already or do we see that happen before our eyes?

MISS W.

She's cold sober at the top of the song.

DC

Cold sober? In the title of the song, the lady is ordering "... another Old-Fashioned, please." We don't know how many she's put away before the curtain went up but since she has no trouble speaking, we can assume she's had at least one and what's your guess ... three cocktails?

MISS W.

If you're asking me, I'm a cheap date. Two drinks and I'm fuzzy. But, at the beginning of the song, she says she's been on the wagon, so I guess you don't say that unless ... (*She pauses a moment.*) No, she's not an alcoholic. Since she mentions the subject only that once, my "educated guess" is that she's probably just started on a diet. That stuff is fattening. And there's something else. You know how, when we do something good for ourselves, we go around boasting about it and telling everybody how they ought to do it, too?

DC

Yes, she does that. Everything is fine except for one thing.

MISS W.

When you need a drink, you need a drink.

DC

By the way, where is she drinking? In her home?

MISS W.

No, she's in a bar, drinking those Old-Fashioneds we talked about. Before the curtain went up she'd been putting away singles but, when the Chorus begins, she changes her mind and makes it a double. That's when we find out what happened to her. She starts telling her tale of woe to the waiter.

DC

Does he have anything to say?

MISS W.

No, but I've always had a sneaking feeling that this is the sort of thing bartenders have to put up with—having to listen to everyone's troubles. His silence is probably his best defense.

DC

But she's talking to the waiter, not to a bartender. In any event, let's get back to our unhappy lady. Can you tell us who left whom?

MISS W.

Why, naturally, he left her.

DC

No politicking, please. Just the facts. *(Laughter from the Class)*

MISS W.

Sorry. There isn't much more to add. Just that once her life was perfection and now it's in ruins. At the finish, telling her story to the waiter has been so painful that she decides against the cocktail and all the fixings, and orders a straight rye.

DC

Very good, indeed. *(Miss W. exits as DC continues)* We are now in possession of the "Who," the "Why," and the "Where" of Miss W.'s "One." The "When" will have to wait until we talk about the "Two." For now, we move on.

His Work

Mr. T. is a young character actor who, by virtue of his physical appearance and the bias of casting directors, lives exclusively in the television world of comedy. DC suggests a lyric by Dorothy Fields that takes him out of baggy pants into pinstripe:

1ST "8"	If I had a cow and a plough and a frau
(A)	How good my life would be
	I'd make a home where I know my heart would rest.
2ND "8"	I could hitch the cow to the plough

(A)   While my frau looked on and smiled at me
    Smiled as she dreamed of the dreams we love the best.
BRIDGE   Dreams about a meadow rolling in the sunlight
(B)   And a field of clover for the pretty cow
    Dreams about a baby laughing at a raindrop
    How do you suppose a new world grows?
LAST "8"   Starting with a cow and a plough and a frau
(A)   It's simply A B C
    I'd plough more land if the cow had children
    We would expand if my frau had children
    Things must be planned for my children's children, now!
CODA   All I need is a cow,
    And a plough,
    And a beautiful frau.

Mr. T., emboldened by Miss W.'s "One" and DC's readiness to help when help is needed, is on stage and eager to begin. DC restrains him in order to give the Class the historical context of the material.

DC
(*To the Class*)

"A Cow and a Plough and a Frau" was written by Dorothy Fields and Morton Gould. For over forty years, Miss Fields wrote her words for the theater and the screen in collaboration with many of our greatest composers. Her first hit, the standard "I Can't Give You Anything But Love," was written in 1928, and well into the decade of the seventies, with Cy Coleman, she was still turning out stunning work in *Sweet Charity* and *Seesaw*. Morton Gould's fame lies solidly among America's better-known serious composers. He wrote only two Broadway scores—for *Billion Dollar Baby* with Comden and Green and *Arms and the Girl* with Miss Fields. Unfortunately, scores die when the shows for which they are written are not "hits." Songs from those scores, even those that are considered gems, disappear into that never-never land of "misses" where they are almost never heard from again. Mr. T.'s song is one of Gould and Field's most felicitous creations. The title is a bit hard to take until one learns that the show is a musical adaptation of the Lawrence Langner and Armina Marshall play *Pursuit of Happiness*. Both the play and the musical take place in eighteenth-century colonial America. The young leading man in the piece is a Hessian, which gave Miss Fields the opportunity to rob from the German to gain a rhyme. For now, we are not concerned with Morton Gould's contribution, but Mr. T. is standing by to tell us what Miss Fields's lyric has to say for itself.

MR. T.

This is a story about a man.

DC

There is no doubt about the narrator's gender?

MR. T.

None whatever.

DC

You are right. How about the ages of the man?

MR. T.

Minimally it's late teens and maximally, well … I had some trouble setting this after I heard you cross-examine Miss W.

DC

I don't see why. Here is a man who fantasizes about having a wife, children, and grandchildren. How old dare he be?

MR. T.

I thought maybe his sixties, at the outside.

DC
(To Mr. T. and the Class)

Good. We'll disregard that "I thought …" When the subject of the extremes of age comes up, we are all agreed that both outer limits will never be ideal. All that concerns us in this case is: Can a man in his six-ties marry, have children, and still live to see his grandchildren? The an-swer would have to be yes. On the other hand and, probably for you, more seemly, how young can he be?

MR. T.

His teens?

DC

Exactly. Again, both ages are allowable but neither one makes us happy. Can you tell the Class why?

MR. T.

Well … if he's in his teens there's no drama. You'd expect him to have those kinds of dreams. If he's in his sixties, you're wondering why he never got off his butt and made them come true.

DC

First rate. That leaves the optimal age?

MR. T.

I think I'm getting the hang of this. My choice would be to go with a guy in his late thirties. That's old enough for him to be getting a little worried about still being alone in his life and not too old to make him come off a psychological misfit.

DC

You certainly are getting the hang of it. *(To the Class)* Some degree of subjectivity always colors your choice of the protagonist's optimal age, but knowing that this will be so should keep you on your toes. Find your justification where it lies—in the lyric. And now, would you tell us where the story takes place?

MR. T.

Anywhere *but* on a farm. If he lived on one, he wouldn't be wishing he had one to live on.

DC

Well put. What about his education and the state of his finances?

MR. T.

There isn't a hint in the lyric to give me a bead on what he's worth. The fact is, a poor man, a not-so-poor man, a not-so-rich man and a rich man—any one of them could sing this song.

DC

I congratulate you. You are right on. And his education?

MR. T.

I couldn't nail that one down, either.

DC

You would agree with me, though, that he is not uneducated. And he has quite a gift for expressing himself—sometimes even poetically.

MR. T.

Well, yes, he does speak well, but poetically? How do you mean?

DC

Surely a man who describes the baby he fantasizes as "... laughing at a raindrop" is not without a sensitivity for the well-chosen phrase?

MR. T.

I see.

DC

There is an archetypal name for this chap. Can you help me?

MR. T.

No problem there. He's a Walter Mitty type.

DC

Exactly. Tell the Class why he would be called that.

MR. T.

He lives in a world of dreams. Every line, or pretty nearly every line, begins with "... If I had a ..."

DC

How about listing those "If I had a's" in the order that he brings them up.

MR. T.

First—it's hard here not to use the exact words of the lyric—he wishes he had a cow, and then a piece of farm machinery to work the land he doesn't have yet, and—I'm still sticking to the order he prefers them in—a wife. So I guess he's a bachelor, right?

DC

A safe guess. As for the order in which he lists his dreams, we can only report it, and give him the benefit of the doubt that this chronology is in the reverse order of its importance to him. But, it is in the next line that we begin to see what his real problem is, don't you agree?

MR. T.

Yes, indeed. He says that if he had those three items, he would finally have peace in his life. That's why I said before that he definitely does *not* live on a farm. From the looks of things, he probably lives in a big city where the rush and the noise make everybody wish they had somewhere they could go to get away from things.

DC

Yes, each line leads to yet another "... If I had a ...," and they seem to get "hotter" as he reveals himself.

MR. T.

I felt that way, too. By the way, that wife he dreams about? Well, he doesn't want just any wife. He wants one who feels the same way he does about living on a farm and working it. Come to think of it, he doesn't say what they'd be planting.

DC

But he does tell us what kind of land he prefers?

MR. T.

Yes. No flat Kansas real estate for him. Hills and dales, not too high or too low, under a perfect sun and even a corner of the farm where that cow—his very first dream—could graze.

DC

Where does that baby come in?

MR. T.

Right now. And, as I said, no colicky baby for him.

DC

Good. After we hear about this perfect baby, he stops the daydreaming to address the audience. Why does he do that?

MR. T.

Well, I think ...

DC

Never mind what you think. All we want to know is what is on *his* mind.

MR. T.

That slipped out. He thinks these...uh...dreams he's been telling us are not that special; that men have always been dreaming them. That's how new worlds begin.

DC

How?

MR. T.

With a cow, a piece of farm equipment, a wife, and then a baby. And soon that cow becomes a herd of cattle, although he doesn't quite say how he worked that one out. And the baby has brothers and sisters, and, as the years go by, they grow up and have their own children.

DC

It is this last fantasy that jerks him back to reality, isn't it?

MR. T.

Yes. Because, you see— (*To the Class*) He doesn't have any of the things he's been telling us about. Not one of them. And you get this spooky feeling that it's getting later and later and if he ever plans on getting started, it had better be soon.

DC

Soon?

MR. T.

Immediately.

DC

Is that it?

MR. T.

Pretty much so. Oh, yes, he repeats the first three dreams—the ones about a cow and a plough, but he adds one more thing he expects his wife to be.

DC

What's that?

MR. T.

Beautiful. She's got to be beautiful. *(The laughter of the Class covers Mr. T.'s return to his seat. DC congratulates him for the good work and concludes the Class with a wrap-up discussion of the "One.")*

DC

I have said that the minimal and maximal ages of the narrator of each of your scripts are the *allowable* ones that will never, by their very definition, be ideal. In Mr. T.'s lyric, were a teenage young man to dream of "... a home where I know my heart would rest," he would know little of the true meaning of those words. It is not his fantasies that are denied him, but the societal restrictions that cage him at the painful age when we are too old to be children and to young to be taken seriously. The boy's minimal age, described by Mr. T. as "ordinary," is too commonplace to engage the interest of the audience. At the other extreme, placing the man in his sixties presents an image of him that the audience can *see*. Questions come to mind: Why has he waited so long? What is this "restless heart" he speaks about? What inhibited him from taking his life into his own hands? The lyric is much too elliptical for comfort. It suggests but it does not inform. So, you see, in both cases, the extremes of age are allowable but, in the sense of their effectiveness at heightening the drama, they are not tolerable.

We know the "Who," the "Why," and the "Where" of the scripts illustrated for us by Miss W. and Mr. T. Each of you can check out your own assigned lyrics to learn the information, which will always be particular to the specific song you are singing. In the case of the "When," every song shares the identical time: It is now. Even better: the *now* of now. Nothing in the theater is duller than the past and the imperfect tense. If a lyric is written about a past event, flash back to "then" and make it "now." We will speak of the importance of this in the following chapter.

The "One" gives you all the facts that are to be found in the lyric. Once you know them you are better able to deal with their significance. The importance of learning a lyric early in the game of mounting a performance runs counter to the theory that holds that dialogue memorized too early inhibits the actor's rehearsal life. It is not my purpose here to reopen that debate except to caution the actor that it is neither wise nor an easy feat to ad lib the words of Sondheim, for example, or at least not when he is in the theater participating in the rehearsals. Noel Coward once defended his habit of going into rehearsal always word perfect: "... I don't worry whether I am getting at the right meaning at this point. When I get up on the stage, the words give me the meaning; you can't know better than the words."

We now know the words. It is time to concern ourselves with their "... right meaning."

12

The "Two"

*Heard melodies are sweet, but those unheard are
sweeter.*

—John Keats

If one, five, twenty, or a hundred actors were asked to do a "One"
on *Hamlet,* it is reasonable to suppose that you would hear
approximately the same story. As we have said, facts are facts. Ask
these same actors what *Hamlet* is *about* and there would be no two
answers alike. This fathomless mystery is elemental to all art. In the
theater it is what compels directors and actors to attempt to fathom it;
and with each new production there will be those who witness it, reject
it on the grounds that this interpretation is not what it is about, and set
out to define it in their own terms. The "Two" you create on your
assigned text will, as in the case of an infinity of Hamlets, be your
subjective understanding of the lyric. It will be a choice you arrive at,
not so much by reading the lyric (the "One"), but by reading into it
what you think it is about (the "Two").

THE "TWO": HOW TO CONSTRUCT IT

The primary function of the "Two" is *to make you move*. Whenever you find you are standing still because what you are saying does not need body language to define it further, you will know that, without a doubt, you are not speaking an active text, which, at least at that moment, and for the purposes of this exercise, is called a "Two." Repeat: *A "Two" is identified only as a verbal statement that makes you move.*

Just as the "One" began with the prescribed sentence: "This is a story about a man … a woman … a boy … or a girl," etc., every "Two" begins with "This is a story about *me*." If a "One" was about a man or a woman, the "Two," depending on who is doing it, will now be about either one or the other gender.

The "Two" starts at zero, eyes focused center, weight planted on both feet, and your hands at your sides. As you begin the sentence, "This is a story about me," you will feel a sense of increasing intensity built into it. The first word, "This," gives specificity to what was general until the moment before you began, and "… is a story" contains a growing fervor that rises to the hottest word in the sentence: "… me." The "zero" you were in on the word "This …" has slowly altered into the physical appearance of the first acting beats that grow out of "… is a story about me."

Following this opening, we will create a subjective script—a dialogue in which only your lines are heard—that includes the following.

1. *To Whom* are you speaking? Name the person, e.g., Fred, Mary, Dr. Smith, Mrs. Jones, Mother. The name should follow the opening sentence: "This is a story about me, Fred"; "This is a story about me, Mother." The choice of your vis-à-vis is not arbitrary. It should be someone who, by virtue of their involvement in your need to play the "Two" to them, furnishes you with conflict. Don't choose someone, then, who wants to hear the tale or, worse, someone who doesn't care whether he or she hears it or not. *Whom* you elect to speak to, at the very top of your "Two" through to its end, will determine how you play the scene. If infidelity is the subject of your "Two," you would boast of it in the locker room to Fred, repent of it to the priest in the confessional, fight to keep it from your wife, and be shamed to have to tell it to your son or daughter. The *To Whom* is your "feed," so choose it to gain the most conflict that, in turn, will energize the physical aspect of your "Two." (The center spot you were working to in the focus exercises in Chapter Nine is now named).

2. *When* is it? At the close of Chapter Ten, I spoke of the *now* of now. It is the present tense that furnishes the scene with its urgency. In the theater, the old saw, "Show them, don't tell them," should be the abiding elemental time signature in which your "Two" cooks. An interesting marginal note: Although the English language has a present narrative tense, we sometimes bypass it and resort to solecism in order to gain and maintain our listeners' involvement in the tales we tell. For example, the following construction:

"I had [the past perfect tense] the strangest experience last night, Dad. The damndest things have been happening [the present perfect tense] to me. I was walking [the imperfect tense] down the street and, out of nowhere, there I am [the present tense] face-to-face with this guy and I says [the vulgarized present tense] to him ..."

If, in our real lives, there is this unconscious compulsion to dramatize the stories we tell, even at the cost of bad grammar, it is even more compelling—and consciously so—in the theater where boredom and not bad sentence structure is at stake. That is why the time is always *now* on stage, and when it is *then* we employ the flashback in order to make the past the present so that we may live it once again, in the "now."

These dramatic verities are no less valid when you sing what you have to say. Your "Two" will reveal incident or characters or even tedious exposition (the less of it the better), but the revelations will always be taking place *now.* The audience may not always hear them in your "Two" but *you* will hear them in your head. You will know what just happened, what is happening, and what possibly will happen as you play the scene from moment to moment. Without this sense of time—this "nowness"—there is no reason to feel urgent about anything.

3. *Where* are you? The "Two" must take place in a specific place. It need not be named but *you* will know where you are. This knowledge can affect the physical life of your "Two." Are you in a library where you must whisper? In a crowded space where you are being jostled? Is it hot or cold? Do you shiver or perspire? Just as the knowledge of what just happened, what is happening, and what possibly will happen is inherent in the *When* of your "Two"—*where* you have just come from, *where* you are, and *where,* after the "Two," you will be going supplies your "Two" with valuable input.

4. *Why* are you telling the "Two?" Do not create a "Two" that lacks provocation. The need to tell it must be absolute.

Don'ts

1. Don't waste time on exposition. Remember: Exposition, by definition, is passive. A "Two" must be active. It is a dialogue, if you will, with all the lines given to you. You may permit the person to whom you are playing to speak in order to reenergize what you are saying, but, since what they say is inaudible to anyone in the audience, never allow them more than a word or two. An example of a "Two" saddled with an excess of exposition:

> "This is a story about me, John. I'm working in that new photography shop on Main and Broadway; you know, the one with the window full of camera equipment. Well, anyway, there's this guy there who's a pain in the neck. I think he's running for crown prince of the place. Always trying to get on the boss's good side while me, I'm coming off like some kind of fool. It's a good job, though. When I'm there a full year, if I make it, I'll be eligible for benefits and then maybe Mary and I can get away for two weeks and take a trip somewhere. Let me tell you, we could sure use a vacation!"

This is banter. It is not a "Two." Your mouth is the only part of you that can be expected to move while you are speaking it. Can it be altered and made to work? Yes. To begin with, make John the man who works in the photography store. As the exposition tells us so tediously, he would furnish us with the perfect antagonist. We can then cut all that information about the shop (where it is, what it sells, and what's in the window) since John knows this as well as the man telling the "Two." By changing the *To Whom* I am speaking and the *Why* I am speaking these words, the "Two" can be made into an active scene between two men who are vying for position and job security. The *Why* can be further strengthened by giving Mary a better reason for that two-week vacation. Has the teller of the "Two" just come from home where Mary told him to "ask for the raise you know you deserve or don't bother to come home at all!" With that ultimatum still ringing in our man's ear, John is an even greater threat. This major alteration of the "Two" may make it unusable but, in the process, you will have discovered what is or isn't a "Two" by learning what does or doesn't create movement.

2. Don't move arbitrarily just to make a "Two" move you. All body language must be organic to the script.

3. Do not lose your Center focus. When you feel it thinning, restate its name to regain its reality for you. You may take your eyes off it when you are impelled to, just as you do when you talk to anyone. A relentless eyeball-to-eyeball focus is as suspect as no focus at all. Remember only that the *To Whom* you are speaking is always Center and may not be permitted to exit until you say so.

4. Don't hone your prose. It has no literary value. It is not going to be published. And once it becomes the subtext of the lyric (the "Three"), it won't even be heard. Think of the "Two" as small talk about a big subject—small talk that will activate body talk. I have heard thrilling "Two's" that were fascinating to listen to but worthless when they were translated into "Three's" (see Chapter Thirteen, The "Three"), and I have heard "Two's" that verged on the nonverbal but moved, in their telling, with a stunning physical language. This is not to say that the body language practiced by the mime is what we are after. Indeed, keep everything you do as true to the reality of the way *you move* as you possibly can. But words, by virtue of their elegance, do not make a "Two." In this regard, shun jokes. You may get your laughs when you do your "Two" but, soon enough, they will be unheard (the "Three") and they will have had no value at all.

5. The "Two," as we have said, is a *subtext* to the lyric of your song. As such, be sure that what you are saying is indicated (not in the actor's use of the word) by what you are doing. If I hear you say "Dammit, it's hot in here!" you should be recognizably affected by the heat. If I hear, "Do you know, I had to run all the way over here? There wasn't a cab anywhere in sight!" I should see you out of breath. When what you *do* is not a manifestation of what you *say,* you are performing a subtext on a subtext to a text. This is a road that leads to madness when you begin to work on your "Three." At that point, the "Two" will appear to create and set the text of the lyric. Do not invent a third voicing.

Of marginal interest: Since the "Two" is a physical manifestation of what you are saying, it should be universally comprehensible. An Englishman, a Czech, or an Australian aborigine should be able to understand a good part of what you say by what he sees. For this reason, when there is a foreigner in the Class, I allow him to speak his "Two" in his mother tongue. In this manner, not only will his body language be his own rather than a once-removed invention but, not surprisingly, the Class and I understand a good portion of what he is saying.

6. Don't use props. Don't call your vis-à-vis on the phone; have him over. No toasting the New Year in with unseen bottles of champagne.

No eating unseen food. Body language is born out of an active need to play the scene. It is not an activity, nor a charade of the "Two."

7. Don't be an artful dodger by inventing someone behind whom you can hide. Again, remember, whenever you sing, it is always *you* who will be singing. Now is a good time to come forward and claim yourself.

8. Don't stage yourself. A "Two" is not a piece of choreography. Don't concern yourself with what you are *doing*; stay true to the "Two." If you say, "Dammit, it's hot in here!" it is only important that it be hot. It does not matter which hand wipes the brow—in fact, you may not wipe the brow at all and, instead, find yourself loosening the collar, fanning the air, or gasping for breath. What is important is this: If it is truly hot, *move* you will. Even body language is subject to a statute of limitations. When you perform a "Two" over and over again, what you do that illustrates how hot it is begins to repeat itself. This is inevitable. To guard against staging yourself, "freeze" the monologue and not its physical appearance.

The most asked question, "How far from the lyric may I go when I create my 'Two?'" is the hardest to answer. I have seen valuable "Two's" that are prosaic equivalents of the subject matter of the poetic lyric and I have seen others that are—at least, verbally—very distant but, when the "Three" is performed, sit on the text with astonishing analogy. Keep in mind that the "Two" will mesh with the lyric all too soon. One need not go far afield of the text unless what it is about fires your creative imagination. The "Two" may then seem distant from the lyric when we hear it, but, when the acting beats that bind it together are laminated onto the words of the song, their physical expression may be right-on antecedents of the words.

Do's

1. In the beginning, while you are still fumbling for a handle upon which to build your "Two," always keep the lyric before you. The more you read it, the closer you will come to understanding what it is about. When you hit on what it is about, you are at the start of the end of your search. In "Make It Another Old-Fashioned, Please," you may feel that:

a. ... this is about self-punishment. Here is a lady who has stopped drinking but, at a moment of profound grief, hurries to a bar in order to anesthetize her pain or, perhaps, her guilt in self-destructive behavior. If this is what you read into the lyric, examine your own history or the conduct of others under stress. Isolate the event or its fictional dramatization, apply the *To Whom, When, Where,* and the *Why* rules of construction, and you will be on your way to creating a viable "Two."

b. Are there other inferences to be drawn from "Make It Another Old-Fashioned, Please"? Of course. It could be about loss; how we fight it, withstand it, and come through it. There is no one who cannot find an experience relative to loss—we have all suffered its pain.

c. Is "Make It Another Old-Fashioned, Please" about drinking? No. You could as well go off a diet as go off a wagon. Just as you do not have to have murdered a king to play Macbeth, you do not have to experience the effects of alcohol to know the meaning of self-punishment.

2. Keep the lyric in front of you as you write your "Two." Better still, write the lyric down and skip three or four lines between each line, using that space to fill in your "Two." In this way, you will be assured that it will always be the lyric that initiates what you write. Fight the impulse to allow the "Two" to tell its story in any way it chooses. *It must be slave to the lyric.*

3. If you feel you need a moment at the top of the "Two" that will help you to set where you are and what is happening—for example, "This is a story about me, Harry. For the last time, put that damned paper down and listen to me!"—allow it. But remember: Give yourself something to *do* while you are verbalizing these opening lines and *keep them short.*

4. Execute the "Two" full out. Experience its physical life at the maximum. Even if it seems to you to be too much, it can and will be pared down later. I do not mean to imply that a "Two" is better for being bigger. In fact, small body language can, by its very density, be "sized," while flailing arms and busy feet may very well signify nothing. However, a combination of disdain for the "hammy" and the need to pull down for the movie and television screens have done the young American actor a disservice. So many actor-singers, with solid training in the first half of the hyphenate billing, are incapable of "taking stage." Their bodies are untrained and unwilling to share, along with their emotional palette, the burden of the work. By asking your "Two" to fulfill itself fully, you will have investigated the outer limits of space displacement. The musical stages upon which you will work are not served by subtlety. (The seating capacity of the Dallas State Fair is 3,420; the Indianapolis Starlight Musical Theater, 4,400; the Kansas City

Starlight Theater, 7,858; and the St. Louis Opera, a whopping 10,117!) Now is the time to bring the physical eloquence of your personal style to the forefront of your thinking.

5. May you use more than one vis-à-vis? Yes. If you are talking to Barbara—your center focus—there may be others on the left and on the right to whom you relate. However, it is important to know, at each moment of your "Two," whom you are addressing. For example:

"This is a story about me, Barbara. There's so much I want to tell you, but that guy over there …
> *(Glancing to the Left)*

… is staring at us. Can't we go inside? Just for a minute? Please? And that moon …
> *(Spotting to right on a higher plane)*

… it's so damned beautiful …
> *(Back to Barbara in Center)*

… I … I just can't keep my mind on what I want to ask you!"

6. You will have to write a short coda to your "Two." If you think of the "Two" as an inner monologue whose acting beats set up *what you are going to say,* its last line would be the one that sets up the last line of the lyric. But there are four bars of music in a Rideout and, with nothing to do, you will find that you will have dropped out of your life in the "Two" and are standing at zero for what seems an unbearable amount of time (see Chapter Fifteen: The "Five"). These last moments that you write for yourself should be designed to "cool" you and simplify your physical life so that, at the last moment of the Rideout, you are at the zero where you began "This is a story about me." For example, picking up the closing moments of a "Two."

"Well, that's how it goes, Harry. One minute I was high up there, had the world right in the palm of this hand, and then, pfft, I lost it all. The money, the job, and worse, she walked out and I haven't seen her since!
> *(Rideout)*

Oh, well, you live and you learn. Next time I won't be such a sucker for an easy buck. You know what I mean, Harry?"
> *(A carefree shrug and … out)*

I tend to think of these added, "cooling" moments in the "Two" as a reverse of its opening: "Me about story a is this …" that gets me back to zero.

7. During that distressing time when you are still searching for a handle for your "Two" but have not yet settled on one, try to keep in mind—while you are still able to do so—that the words of your song and your "Two" should be consonant in tone. A Cole Porter lyric will not sit well on a heavy, Chekhovian "Two" or an overly elegant subtext mesh with the unaffected simplicity of Irving Berlin's words.

8. Must a "Two" make narrative sense? Not necessarily, although I find it easier to perform one that does. Here is an example of a "Two" with no continuity—for that matter, no story points are made at all—nor is there one consistent focus:

(Center)
"This is a story about me, Doctor Fardel.
(In a growing rage)
I've been sitting out there ...
(Indicating the waiting room in Right wing)
... in your waiting room for over an hour. Why the hell does your nurse give out appointments that no one takes seriously?
(Left focus—warming with affection)
I was only kidding, Mary. I *like* your dress ...
(Right focus—growing puzzlement)
... that car? Nope, that's not for me, Mr. Jordan. Why should I buy a gas-guzzler like that? I just need wheels to get around town.
(Center—with deep pleasure)
Hey, Ma! You made my favorite! Coconut cream pie! I sure hope you didn't invite a lotta people. I'd hate to have to share it with ...
(Staying center, but with growing shock)
Liz said she was coming? But she would've let me know!
(Mounting anger)
Wait a minute! You haven't been opening my mail?! You promised!"

This "Two" will physicalize with no difficulty but, without continuity and narrative development, the actor must slither in and out of the "beats" of a script that is being created to serve as a subtext to a lyric. Since each line has no pertinence to what precedes or follows it, graceful transitions would be difficult to maneuver. It is less complicated to deal with a "Two" that unwinds through a series of related story points, directed to one antagonist out front. Furthermore, remember that when the "Two" becomes a "Three," it is a good deal easier to deal with a coherent subtext. But I am reminded of the fable of the parents who, as they are leaving for the evening, warn their children not to put peas up their noses. Of course, as soon as they are gone, the children, never having heard of the entertainment, run to try it—with dire results. You may try this kind of "Two" but if you have too much trouble pulling it off, go back to the reliable *To Whom, When, Where,* and *Why.*

At this point in the class, there is always a time-lag due to a combination of confusion, anxiety, misapprehension, and the search for a handle for the "Two." Inevitably, the first intrepid actor agrees to show the opening moments of his work, preferring to test the waters of my approval before risking a dive into rejection. Once I see his seminal ideas, I am able to lead him further toward a more valuable script. There is something about a "Two" that tends to terrify. As long as the exercise remains described and not witnessed, the Class flounders. But as soon as the first performer breaks through, the blockage is breached and what seemed opaque becomes clear to everyone who sees it.

DC now reprises the opening procedure for the Class. When you first stand in the Center, focus front and begin, "This is a story about me ..." at zero. We are picking up where we left off at the end of the Vamp before we began to sing but first, some Don'ts and Do's:

Don'ts

1. Don't get into position until you are ready to start. You should be standing Center but remain easy. Deal with the time you need for preparation. When you are ready, and not a second sooner:

    a. spot Center;

    b. follow with weight on both feet;

    c. place your hands at your sides and begin "This is ..." etc.

Don't let your eagerness to do the "Two" dictate when you begin.

2. Just as I recommend that you not begin until you are ready, it is important that when you have come front and are in position to begin—begin. If you stand at zero, staring front for more than a moment, at the most, you will start to petrify. Once your focus recognizes Center and the above activities have followed in the wake of that recognition of the theater's presence, know that you are almost at that time when the Stage Manager will call, "Curtain Up."

3. Don't *act* when you hear yourself saying "This ..." The "Two" does not begin to physicalize itself until you are at the word "... story." Until then, the Center focus is a spot that is not yet personalized.

4. Don't speak the sentence too quickly. If anything, start it slowly so that you feel the "white" of "this is ..." changing to the "pink" of "... a story" that builds to the "red" of "... about me." When the line is spoken too rapidly, the moment-to-moment color transitions will be rushed and jerky. You are creating a life that changes the Center focus from a nameless dot out front to a human being who, by virtue of its birth, affords you what you need: *reaction.*

Do's

1. In the exercises in Chapter Seven, we timed going from *something* to *nothing* just before we began to sing. Now we are reversing the procedure by starting from *nothing* (zero) to the *something* that is the first physical manifestation of your "Two." To resist the urge—and to resist it is not easy—to use only the upper quadrants of your body while your feet stay nailed to the floor, train yourself to begin the physical life of your "Two" (somewhere around "... story about") by reacting first with your feet and then continue on up until not only your hands are involved but all of you is in the scene right from the start of the "Two." In December 1976, the distinguished actress Eva Le Gallienne gave an interview to the *Los Angeles Times.* In it, she made this insightful comment:

> "I always say to actors, don't put corks on your fingers. So many of them stop here," she said, indicating her hands, "instead of letting it go on like a ray. An actor should be bigger than his body."

I, too, am concerned with these corks. They live at the ends of your fingers, as well as in your hips, legs, and feet. Uncorking happens when you think *feet first.*

2. A valuable trick: give your vis-à-vis, somewhere around "... a story ..." a cue to which you can react. It may be a line you give him or her to say, or something they are doing that provokes the opening beats of your "Two." Later, in the Performance section of this volume, we will see that, for the performer, the first line printed in the sheet music of a song is actually the second line—the first being the unheard cue-line that only the singer hears.

DIALOGUES

Her Work

Miss W. is eager to begin. DC asks her to go straight to Center stage, but not to begin.

MISS W.

It's so hard to stand up here doing nothing.

DC

If you think, "This is where I stand and do nothing," you will do nothing badly. It is true that you are up there to sing a song. How you do that is not one whit more important than learning how *not* to sing a song before you have one to sing. Turn a little away from that dead-front, head-on stance. Get rid of any feeling of self-consciousness. After all, you will have to deal with these moments at an audition before you sing. Does this make any sense to you?

MISS W.

It's very strange, but this is the first time I understand what you mean about not doing anything specific before you *do* the song. May I try it again?

DC

Of course. I remember reading Tyrone Guthrie's response to the question, "If you had to give just one word of advice to an actor before he began a scene, what would it be?" Said Dr. Guthrie, "Take a breath." So—take a breath before you begin.

Miss W. takes a breath and then slowly, without stiffening, she begins to experience herself. No more inventing activities like clothes-adjusting and rearranging—just *being*. The class and DC are enthusiastic. He asks her to continue. In good time, her eyes come front and focus Center, her base moves into position, and her hands follow suit as they go to her sides.

MISS W.

"This is a story about me, Max."

DC
(*Interrupts*)

Do it again. The "Two" arrived too early. You were already in it—doing something—as you said the second word. Easy does it. Don't forget that it is you who creates that life out front, in this case, Max. Don't rush his birth.

Miss W. tries again, but this time the "Two" begins too late. But, having timed it to both extremes, her third try hits it right on the mark.

MISS W.
(*Elated*)

I really felt that! It was the smoothest transition I think I ever achieved. I mean, going from nothing through to the end of that silly sentence.

DC

Try it again. The mechanics of the exercise will always be the same. If you can do it once, you should have no trouble doing it over and over again.

Miss W. tries it a second time and it is clear to the Class that whatever interior process she has been using not only works but is capable of reprise. She has captured the rising arc of "This is a story about me."

Because the "Two" is a visual exercise, the reader cannot understand it as comprehensively when it is on paper and not something seen. I have written her "Two" side by side with Porter's lyric and parenthisized acting "beats," adverbs, adjectives, and all descriptive phrases—retaining what any good director would delete from the script—in order to help the reader visualize the physical appearance of Miss W.'s "Two." You may want to try it for yourself. Beware of playing results. The "Two" will stay alive if you deal with its action. Cause and effect occur in that order. Without the first there is no second.

The "Two"	The Lyric
This is a story about ... (*Zero*) (*Max mentions Miss W.'s weight*) ... about me, Max ... (*She is amused and placates him.*) All right, all right, so I put on a little weight. OK. OK. Maybe more than a little. But smoking ... smoking, Max, is worse! You listen to me ...	Since I went on the wagon

(*She watches him light a cigarette, and then, with dire warning in her voice*) … that weed'll kill you … I know!	I'm certain drink is a major crime.
But look at me, Max. Three months without a cigarette and I'm Miss America. A little heavier, but a winner!	For when you lay off the liquor
(*She takes a deep breath and runs her hands along her chest.*) Clear lungs, no headaches, no throat-aches—and food, Max! You can't believe what it tastes like!	You feel so much slicker,
(*Her hands have arrived at hip level. She looks down and then back to Max.*) So, all right, what's fifteen pounds? I put 'em on, I can take 'em off!	Well, that is most of the time.
(*A bit nervous, she fixes her hair in an effort to appear casual.*) But, never mind that, Max. The audition. I want to hear what they thought about my reading. No, tell me all of it. (*A timorous, girlish shrug*) Frankly, I thought it went quite well.	But there are moments, Sooner or later,
Of course, (*A bit edgy*) I was a little shaky. You know, the added weight, and all. God! How I hate those cold readings! But, Max … … be a friend for once … and not an agent. Please! Tell me! The truth, Max …	When it's tough I've got to say, Not to say: "Waiter,
(*Supplicating*) Stop the hemming and hawing …	Make it another Old-Fashioned, please.

This job's so important, Max. I mean, all this self-improvement—shaking the weed and all, it's ... well, I need the work, Max. You can see that, can't you?	Make it another double Old-Fashioned, please.
(*Growing indignation*) That's what irritates me, really irritates me. There you sit, like some complacent, smug little ...	Make it for one who's due to join the disillusioned crew,
Oh, I can't ... I just can't face this endless rejection. (*She slowly surrenders to complete exhaustion.*) Is this what my life's to be about, Max? Thank you's, maybe next times, too old's, too young's, and unemployment insurance?	Make it for one of love's new refugees.
(*Glowingly, and she recollects*) Lord! What I'd give to have just a little of it back! It was always so full of light at the beginning!	Once, high in my castle, I reigned supreme.
(*Reaching up with joy.*) That feeling of infinite possibilities with no limits! Anything can happen and you know ...	And oh! What a castle!
(*She touches her breast gently.*) ... you know right here that it will.	Built on a heavenly dream.
(*She sags, exhausted once again.*) All right. (*Resigned*) Tell me, right now ... where I stand ...	Then, quick as a light'ning flash
(*Hands up as if to shield a blow*) I didn't get it, did I? (*Shaking her head to corroborate*	That castle

On Singing Onstage

his silent "no")	began to crash!
(Quick change) Oh, forget it! The lousy part was only twelve lines ...	So, make it another Old- Fashioned,
and no damned good to begin with!	please!
(She pivots and starts to leave, and *then turns.)* Max, how about my buying us both a dinner, tonight?	Leave out the cherry
We'll start with drinks and not count one damn calorie!	Leave out the orange,
And end in a blaze of anything flambé'd!	Leave out the bitters,
(She has a second thought.) Oh, and Max ... can I bum one of your cigarettes?	Just make it a straight rye!"
(Rideout) *(She smiles timidly, puts out her hand* *for the cigarette, and ... out).*	

DC

A most interesting "Two." Would you tell the class how you constructed it so that they can hear it from one of their own?

MISS W.

There isn't much to say except that I do think what you said about reading the lyric over and over again and always having it in front of you as you go along writing the "Two" is very important. Your warning about the "Two" wanting to go its own way was so true.

DC

How did you hit on that handle?

152

MISS W.

Well as I read and reread the lyric I came to think of it as a story about failure and how it can seduce you into surrendering to weakness. Maybe this song and my life right now have something in common. (*The Class laughs.*) Agent problems, television commercial interviews, and all the barbarism of the whole damned scene and then, quite suddenly, I had my hook when it hit me that I had just recently given up smoking. It was strange, one minute I had nothing and the next minute it all fell into place.

DC

Very good. Everything you've said we both know the rest of the Class will experience as each one comes closer and closer to nailing down his "Two." May I make a few suggestions that will sharpen the inner life of your "Two" and help to increase the size of its physical appearance? That is, after all, what this exercise is all about.

MISS W.

Of course. Anything!

DC

Who is Max? We know he is an agent and, in the "Two," your agent. But that is his occupation and not *who* he is. Perhaps, purely as the writer of the "Two," if you somehow sensed that he was uninterested in your career and probably planning to get rid of you by ending your contract with his agency, you as the actor of the "Two" would have more grist for your mill. Also, although there is, in the *When*, a sense of nowness in the work, it could be made even more to live in the instant. Could you have done the audition just that morning, forcing him to call to find out how well or poorly you did? Right now. You see, you are past due on the payments on your car and you've been planning on this job for the money to get that nightmare off your back. This would have the added value of heightening the *Why* of the "Two." Finally, the next time I see it, would you perform with a deeper sense of urgency by not thinking in the simple or even the comparative, but in the superlative degree? Do you know what I mean?

MISS W.

I understand. Angry and angrier are not as valuable as angriest.

DC

Exactly.

MISS W.

I think, on the bottom line, I'm worried that I'm going to come off like one of those quick cuts in a silent Russian movie. Suddenly, there he is, the czar's murderer, twice as big as life.

DC

What you are forgetting is that you are a splendid actress whose work in this studio is not at the mercy of a film cutter. I am not asking you to give up what you already know you know. And as for today, what you know has shown us a performance of a first-rate "Two." You deserve a hand. (*The Class responds and a happy Miss W. exits.*)

His Work

A week later, Mr. T. is ready to show the class his "Two" on the lyric of "A Cow and a Plough and a Frau."

MR. T.

I don't think you'll have to help me with the first sentence. I took the notes you gave Miss W. and I think I've got it down pat.

Mr. T. is as good as his word. His *at ease* in Center stage, arrival at the Center focus, and the delivery of "This is ... etc ." is executed with grace. He proceeds without interruption from DC.

The "Two"	The Lyric
This is a story about me, Captain. (Zero) (*The Captain looks up from his desk, unhappy with the interruption— an inquiring "Yes?"*) (*Sheepish*) Sir, Sgt. Blackstone said ...	
	If I had a cow
(*He kicks his foot, "Skippy" fashion.*)	

154

... that this would be a good time for me ...	
	and a plough
(*A rush of courage*) ... to make my request to be in Special Services.	
	and a Frau
(*Warming up*) When I heard I was drafted, Sir, I said to myself, Freddie, I said, the place for you is in Special Services!	How good my life would be
Hell! You could do what you know and be making a real contribution while you're doing it!	I'd make a home where I know my heart would rest.
(*With growing excitement*) Ya' know that old movie house near Camp Funsten ... ?	I could hitch the cow to the plough
(*Losing himself and all military demeanor*) Boy! What a theater that'd make!	While my Frau looked on and smiled at me.
Oh, just close your eyes, Sir! (*Doing the same—really "in" it*) I can see it now!	Smiled as she dreamed of the dreams we love the best.
(*Bending down, arms spread, as though raising the curtain himself*) The curtain goes up ...	Dreams about a meadow
(*Rising, with growing ecstacy*) ... the lights ... come up ...	rolling in the sunlight

(*Sweeping his arm from R to L*) … and the entire First Infantry Division Band marches on playing "Everything's Coming Up Roses"!	And a field of clover for the pretty cow.
(*He stops as he sees the Captain's consternation; quickly changing to mend his fences.*) No good, huh? (*A moment for thought*) I know what I could do! I could read some poetry … maybe …	Dreams about a baby
(*Off in his own world*) … like … Edna St. Vincent Millay!	Laughing at a raindrop.
(*Sees Captain shaking his head, "No"; joins him in the negative head-shake.*) Well, maybe it's not such a good idea.	How do you suppose
(*"No" shake changes to a "yes" nod.*) It doesn't have to be a theater.	a new world grows?
(*He turns away, fighting for his life as he tries desperately to come up with another idea.*)	Starting with a cow and a plough and a Frau
(*He snaps his fingers as an idea is born. Runs back to C.*) I got it! A traveling mobile unit!	It's simply A B C
It's all so simple! We could do a morality play.	I'd plough more land if the cow had children
(*Off on a creative binge again*) Better yet! We could do Macbeth!	We would expand

	if my Frau had children
(*Victorious exaltation*) "Birnham Wood …	
	Things must be planned
… comes to Dunsinane" between the tanks!	
	for my children's children
(*Sees Captain looking at him as though he were mad. Joy slowly turns to weak fear.*)	
	now!
(*Picking up the pieces*) All you'd have to do, Sir, is sign …	
	All I need is a cow
(*Pointing to paper on Captain's desk*) … so I could get …	
	and a plough
… into Special Services.	
	and a beautiful Frau.
(*Rideout*) … Please … (*Destroyed by his failure, he waits a moment in embarrassment, then turns to leave.*)	

The class applauds spontaneously. DC waits for silence.

DC

We are all in agreement. It is a fine "Two." I have a feeling that the Class has been more affected by its verbal statement than by the original physical language you use. Original, of course, to everyone but you. I imagine this is a slice taken from your autobiography?

MR. T.

I have to be honest. I fought like the devil to keep away from that sort of thing, but every "Two" I came up with I'd invent body language to

157

go with it. Then I remembered you had said the purpose of the "Two" is not only to make me move but to make me move the way *I* move. As soon as that hit me, I was more comfortable dealing with, as you say, a slice out of my life.

DC

I guess, and correctly, I imagine, that you decided this script was about a loser?

MR. T.

Yes. Right from the start, I felt he was a dreamer who never gets out of his rut and makes his dreams happen.

DC

What I like particularly about your "Two" is its poignancy and the effectiveness of its revelations. We witness them at the exact moment that they are revealed to you. (*To the Class*) Remember: this is the last time I will know what is on your mind when I see and hear you sing. A well-known singer once said to me, "I have many imitators, but no one knows what I'm thinking." What is important is to make certain that, as Mr. T. has said, your thinking is *your* thinking. We all could imitate the outer appearance of his "Two" but only he, having been misassigned in the army, knows the complicated and painful thought processes that inform his body in the unique way we have seen.

MR. T.

I have to admit that this didn't happen just as you heard it. There's a lot of fiction in there because the lyric does manipulate the "Two" as you go along constructing it.

DC

Yes, the "Two" is the support, the spine of the lyric—but when you are *writing* the "Two" it will always be the lyric (the text) that invokes it (the subtext). In your case, I don't see you having any difficulty fitting it onto Miss Field's words because her words have so obviously decreed the fit. (*To the Class*) It is time to do just that. Let us move on, then, to the "Three."

13

The "Three"

Suit the action to the word, the word to the action.
—William Shakespeare

THE "THREE":
THE LYRIC AND THE "TWO" COME TOGETHER

Mastery of the "Three" gives credence to the general notion that the technical study of a subject tends to increase in difficulty. However, it is of some comfort to learn that once the performer conquers the early sense of defeat the complexity of the exercise inspires, he may rest safe in the knowledge that, from here on, the process of leveling off begins. All technique is laid in and only practice remains. Like any work that calls for coordination, the "Three," once learned, is never forgotten, but the learning of its mechanics can be maddening. Since it is the manifestation of the "Two" (the physicalized subtext to a lyric) laminated onto the *spoken* text (the lyric), it requires a special kind of concentration. Two distinct and separate tracks are meshing and, at the same time, resisting collision. Where the difficulty lies is the very element that gives it its beauty: *The physical life of the "Two" must always precede the words,* each "beat" of the "Two" giving the visual appearance that quite literally sets up the line of the lyric to which it relates. Another way to describe what, if it could be seen, would be immediately understandable: I think of the "Three" as arcs of thought (the "Two") and speech (the lyric) that intersect, the speech following the thought so as to give the impression that it is the steady unfolding of the "Two" that is *seen* to precipitate each line of the *heard* lyric. One *thinks* the "Two," then *speaks* the lyric in a continual flow that moves without jerks, stops, and starts. It is admittedly a difficult business. An image that may help to visualize the process: Imagine the "Two" moving like a motorboat, with the lyric following in the wake it creates. (In the preceding chapter, the "Two" was printed so as to give the reader a visual aid to understanding the out-of-synch timing required in the proper performance of the "Three." Each line of the "Two" was raised above the line of the lyric to which it relates.)

The meld of the "Two" onto the lyric is more easily accomplished if you follow these Don'ts and Do's:

Don'ts

1. Don't discard the opening line: "This is a story about me … ." At least, not yet. It is still to be thought of as the opening of your "Two." We need a starting line that affords a smooth transition from you standing on a stage with nothing on your mind into you starting to sing without any audible cue and with no apparent loss of grace and style. More to the point, you have something so important on your mind that you not only want to but must sing about it. At that point when "This is a story about me …" is no longer required as a prosthesis, the line will fade away out of disuse. Until then, the "Three" must begin, as did the "Two," with eyes focused front and Center, base supported equally on both feet, and hands at sides. All we *hear* is the lyric; all you *think* is the "Two" as it has always begun.

2. Don't pay lip-service to your "Two" now that it is not heard. The "Three" should be a ninety-nine and nine-tenths commitment to your "Two" with only one-tenth of one percent of your concentration given to the lyric. To make sure that you do not give short shrift to the "Two," *do not speak too soon.* Nothing will kill your "Two" faster than your mouth. Wait until the arc of the "Two" that relates to what you are going to say is *fully on you before you begin to speak the line to which it relates.*

3. Whenever I am asked if one cuts or shortens a "Two" when it becomes a silent, supportive element of the "Three," I always cross my fingers and say, "Never!" But, after all, the "Two" when it was verbalized was in prose. Now you will be sustaining it as a life that supports poetic speech. If alteration is required, think of it as less a question of cutting than of condensing, of compressing into an essence of what you are playing rather than a surgical removal of something that may well damage the subtle elements of the "Two"—moments that gave it its transitional flow. Although at any given moment the actual appearance of the "Two" may alter somewhat, I am always aware that A cannot proceed to C without passing through B.

4. Of course, there is the other side of the coin. When the "Two" is played *exactly* as it appeared when it was a simple monophonic "Two," you may look like you are stuck in a dumb-show when you are working a stereophonic "Three." Overdedication to every single move you were accustomed to play in your "Two" is as destructive to your "Three" as mindless cutting can be. If your "Two" spoke about how uncomfortable you are in the heat, you do not have to play the full physical alphabet of what "being hot" looks like. If I see you hot, start to speak your lyrics. But, again, don't begin to speak until you are recognizably hot.

5. Resist the temptation to elocute the lyric. Don't recite it. Don't line-read it. Don't even project it. Whisper it. It is of no great importance that others hear what you are saying. The "Three" is *not a verbal exercise*. Because its only concern is timing the "Two" to the lyric, that is all that should concern you.

Do's

1. A "Three," a "Four" (see Chapter Fourteen), and a "Five" (see Chapter Fifteen) are, in their playing, all "Twos." In order to give as much concentration as you can to your "Two," learn and memorize the lyric backwards and forwards. "Go up" on the words and your "Two" will disintegrate before your eyes. It always saddens me when I see an actor murder his "Two" in order to deliver a word-perfect lyric. On the other hand, nothing cheers me more than a well-performed subtext timed to the delivery of a lyric that, if it is not always word perfect, ad libs for a moment until it can get back on the track.

2. Keep your focus alive. If you feel it fading, silently repeat its name. By now it must be clear to the reader that Mary, Dad, Fred, and Dr. Fardel are all names that define for you the continuous presence of the audience. A "Two," a "Three," a "Four," a "Five"—and every song you will ever sing—belongs to them.

3. Although the pianist is still absent, remember to play out the final beats of your "Two" that follow the last line of the lyric. They will live in the Rideout. When music rejoins the exercise on a "Five," it will all make sense to you. For now, disregard the sensation of nonsense they tend to provoke and play out all the way to the end of your "Two."

4. Pay careful attention to the transitions that lead you out of and into each arc of the "Two." The "Three" will look like a silent movie only when:

   a. you are not fully alive in each moment of the "Two."

   b. your transitions are not elegantly performed.

5. I have allowed the actor-singer a short expositional reference at the top of his "Two." Now it must be cut. For example:

"This is a story about me, Dan. What do you think you're doing? Climbing up the fire escape, opening my bedroom window and coming in here like some thief in the night?! You've got to get out of here! The cops'll be here any minute!"

At the top of her "Two," this lengthy description of what Dan has done before he showed up in her bedroom allowed for a slow—very slow—build. In a "Three" it is expendable. The "Two" should now read and play:

"This is a story about me, Dan. You've got to get out of here! The cops'll be here any minute!"

There is no less shocked outrage but now it is compressed to forestall the silent movie I spoke about in the Don'ts, Number 4.

It can be seen that the dialogues we have been using in which DC and the student, working together, rapidly improve the quality of performance are pure literary montage. No one I have ever taught is able to do a "Three" with expertise the first time around. The subtleties of timing, the fluency of responses to commands (the "Two") received from that part of the brain that instructs the motor system, and, lastly, the seamless spinning out of the "Two" from its initial beginning, "This is a story, etc." moving *always in advance of the spoken lyric,* right through to the end of the Rideout—all of these elements require serious practicing of the "Three," over and over again, to perfect an effortless performance. Relevant to that achievement, a quote of Bertolt Brecht to his company, the Berliner Ensemble, in advance of their first season on the London stage: "Our playing needs to be quick, light, strong. *This is not a question of hurry, but of speed, not simply of quick playing, but of quick thinking."* (The italics are mine.)

Final note: As the work becomes increasingly easier to accomplish without discernible effort, you come to realize that all of life is, more or less, a "Three." Much as lightning precedes the sound of the thunder it creates, mysterious impulses may spike what we say with a physical language—often disparate to what the listener hears—a language that moves ahead of our speech as much to decorate it as to indicate what we really mean. Here is a case in which art mirrors nature. But, as I said at the beginning of this chapter, not without a struggle.

14

The "Four"

Do not commit your poems to pages alone—sing them,
I pray you.

—Virgil

THE "FOUR": SINGING THE "THREE" IN FREE METER

The "Four" should be thought of as a way station between speech spoken and songs sung. To begin with, the accompanist has returned and taken his place at the piano, where he will be found from here on to forever.

The "Four," in the original series of exercises, was a late arrival. The "Three" moved on to what is now the "Five" (then called the "Four"), in which the actor-singer played his "Two" as always, while singing the song as written in the sheet music—the melody and rhythm faithfully observed by both him and the pianist (see Chapter Fifteen: The "Five"). However, it was soon evident that the radical adjustment from speech rhythms to the tempi and pitches that singing requires made concentration on the "Two" almost impossible. The "Four" became the compromise: The melody was allowed in but the time signature was barred entrance. Free to sing *just* the tune in the rhythms of spoken speech immediately unburdened the performer and gave the "Two" a chance to breathe. In the "Four," then, the accompanist cues in the start of each new line with one note, a *Bell-tone*, to keep the musical performance on course. The following Don'ts are of particular importance.

Don'ts

1. The Bell-tones are not an order to sing. They are there so that *when* you need the starting note of a line, it is in the air. But you are still fighting for the life of your "Two." The pianist may be required to play the Bell-tone more than once if he feels you may have missed it but, in a "Four," he waits on *you* and never, the reverse.

2. Don't sing out in full voice or emotionalize the vocal line of the song. Just as it does in a "Three," when you recite or line-read the lyric, belting out the melody will suffocate the "Two." Remember: There are no eighth-notes, quarter-notes, half-notes, whole-notes, rests, or bar signs to contend with—just the whispered pitch levels the composer placed on the words. Keep reminding yourself that this is not a vocalization of the song.

3. Don't sustain notes. Just as you spoke the lyric in your "Three," softly sing it in your "Four."

Do's

1. Do think of the "Four" as visually matching the "Three." A film of a "Four" would superimpose exactly on a film of the "Three" provided there was no sound track.

2. Learn the melody so well that your need of the Bell-tones is minimal. The pianist is there to keep you informed of the next pitch—when you need it—but if your "Four" is playing well, a missed note, here and there, is of no major importance.

3. Just as in the "Two" and the "Three," play the beats of the Rideout, even though the last note of the song is not held in this exercise.

15

The "Five"

> *A translation is no translation, he said, unless it will give you the music of a poem along with the words of it.*
>
> —John Millington Synge

THE "FIVE": THE SONG AND THE "TWO" COME TOGETHER

The "Five" is the last of the technical exercises taught in my Studio. It brings into play the remaining elements that, until now, have been held at bay. The playing of the "Two" is still of primary importance, but now the Bell-tones in the "Four" give way to the full melodic, harmonic, and rhythmic accompaniment of the published song.

Before he performs the "Five," the actor-singer is convinced his "Two" cannot move fast enough to stay ahead of the sung lyric and still manage to remain organic. But it can and it will.

Before he performs the "Five," the actor-singer is convinced that a 4/4 time signature will wrench his "Two" into 4/4 acting. But it won't and it doesn't. (DC makes it clear to the pianist that a slower accompaniment is the better part of charity.)

Before he performs the "Five," the actor-singer is convinced that his "Two" will have to be pared down in order to squeeze even a fraction of it into the spaces (the "Air") between the lines. But it needn't be and it mustn't be.

How, then, does the "Two" survive, now that it no longer dictates its own tempos? With no trouble at all if you observe the following guidelines:

Don'ts

1. Don't linger or allow yourself to get too comfortable at any moment in the by-now accustomed "beats" that make up your "Two." The operative phrase in a "Five": It's always later than you think.

2. Don't indulge in reactions to what you are singing. What you are *going* to be singing is only a split-second away; your "Two" must be a split-second ahead of *that.*

Do's

1. Do think of your "Two" as a series of motel stopovers you check into and out of in order to get an early start.

2. Do learn to let go of what you are *playing* as you hear yourself nearing the end of the line you are *singing.*

3. Do remember that practice makes a "Five" better, if not perfect. On the first try, it will feel a bit like patting your head and rubbing your stomach at the same time. After a while, coordination begins to gain the upper hand. When it all clicks into place—as it does for everyone—you will be astonished at the ease with which you juggle the two tracks of subtext and text.

DIALOGUES

Her Work

Miss W. is ready.

DC

Before you begin, let me tell you and the Class where "... This is a story about me ..." fits into your ad-lib Vamp. Do you recall the first exercise we performed in the Vamp? You were at ease and then you nodded to your accompanist to begin and returned to a general lateral focus into the theater. Somewhere around the downbeat of the third bar of the Vamp, you came front to make Center your specific focus choice.

At that point, your base moved as you adjusted your weight onto both feet, your hands came to your sides, one at a time and, finally, after waiting out the three beats that follow the "sting," you began to sing.

MISS W.

I remember it as well as my own name. (*The Class responds knowing only too well how much rehearsal the work requires.*)

DC

Bear with me. After today, we are done with technique and you will be singing just for the joy of it. No more mechanics, I promise you. For now, back to the "Five." Only one change has to be made to the above sequence: That Center focus, until today, has been nameless—the target at which you aimed your song. Now, at the top of the third bar it will receive "This is a story ... etc." in your "Two," the birthplace of Max, your agent. Remember, don't rush. You will have all the time you need—more than you were prepared for—because your Vamp is in ad lib, and, added to the time available to you, will be the three beats of silence that follow the "sting." Your goal is to move smoothly from "zero" through the opening moments of your "Two" before the first sung-words of the Verse. In your case, if I remember correctly, your subtext began with an admission that you had put on some weight. Am I right?

MISS W.

Yes, because I've noticed he isn't too pleased about it.

DC

Good. Let me warn you that the first performance of a "Five" will always move haltingly. As an aid—and since I know your subtext (the "Two")—I'll cue you whenever I think you are too slow. Think of me as your timer. When you hear me, know that your "Two" is sluggish. Pick up its tempo by picking up the tempo of your thinking. Do I make myself clear?

MISS W.

Let's hope I won't need that crutch.

DC

You will. What is more, you will crave it. But let's begin.

Miss W. takes a moment before she nods to the pianist and deals with the Vamp with no trouble. *Unheard*, we see: "This is a story about me, Max"; *heard* is Cole Porter's "Make It Another Old-Fashioned, Please." When she is late in picking up the cues of her "Two," DC throws them at her. She stays alert, crops what was slowing her down, and reaches the Rideout. As she holds the last note on the word "... rye," DC, like a dispatcher in an airport control-tower, brings her down with: "... All right ... reach out now for the cigarette, stay above the landing strip. Don't come down ... not just yet. OK, give in to the feeble admission of failure ... and out." She is at zero just as the pianist plays the final chord of the four-bar Rideout. The Class is as exhausted as Miss W.

DC

Not bad. Not bad at all. Could you risk trying it and timing it without my help?

Unprompted, Miss W. finds her own rhythms that feed out the "Two" in tandem to Cole Porter's unyielding 4/4 time signature. She is allowed to do it more than once and, with each run-through, the blending acquires more polish. This time, the Class, far from being exhausted, gives her a well-deserved hand. Miss W., heady with achievement, turns the stage over to Mr. T.

His Work

As before, Mr. T. has benefited from watching Miss W. break the new ground.

DC
(*After cuing him through the first performance*)

That was a little ragged, I'm afraid.

MR. T.

I'm thrown when I hear you cuing me in different places than I've rehearsed.

170

DC

I know. It can be confusing. One of the problems you are experiencing is not uncommon. When the physical "business" in your "Two" needs more music, Mr. Gould does not give you enough. When he supplies a longer "fill," you don't have enough "Two" to play through it. But this is easily remedied. Let's take the walkaway—the one that sets up the second half of the lyric, beginning with "Starting with a Cow and a Plough and a Frau." (The reader may find it helpful to follow these directions by referring to Mr. T.'s "Two" in Chapter Twelve, pp. 154–157.) In your "Two," "Three," and "Four," when you could take as much time as you cared to, you walked three or four steps to the R, away from Center, as you struggled to get another idea. Are you with me?

MR. T.

Oh yes, but I'd hate to give that up. I need it and, frankly, I like it.

DC

You won't have to give it up, but, with only two beats allowed you in the music—two quarter-note beats—we have to "shape" it a little. That walkaway must be pared down to a pivot and a quick return. There isn't time for even one step. Just turn and make it appear as if you are going to walk away, but come right back with the new idea that accompanies the fingersnap as you sing "It's simply A B C."

MR. T.

I think that'll be a lot easier. I was trying to keep the walkaway by telling myself I had to have time to get the idea for the mobile unit doing Macbeth.

DC

I think, too, that you were growing a little too fond of that moment. Let's see how little we need to make it work.

Mr. T. tries the pivot turn, returning front almost immediately as he grabs for the new idea that gives life to the fingersnap. The maneuver, forced to live in the two beats allowed by the composer, improves with each try.

DC

Better. I think it would be better still if you start the preparation for the pivot a beat or two sooner in the line: "... Starting with a Cow and a Plough and a Frau." You've been waiting until the last word, "Frau," to begin it. See if you can push it a little ahead to "... *and* a Frau."

As instructed, Mr. T. works the pivot earlier in the line, and the "Five", now that the "business" is less rushed, moves more smoothly. The Class applauds.

DC

Very good. Keep working it again and again. It is a perfect example where the need to shape the outer appearance of a piece of "business" takes precedence over its inner truth. First, educate your motor responses—which side shall I pivot on? On which foot is my weight in order to execute the pivot? Once this is laid away, you can go back to a more artistic performance, knowing that it will be artful, as well. (*To the Class*) We have talked about the essential difference between the staging of a play and a musical. The first develops and achieves its shape, during rehearsals, through the slow addition of the contributions of the director and the actors. In the musical theater, the reverse is standard procedure: The shape is attended to first. Run-throughs of Act One are not uncommon as early as the third day of rehearsals, with Act Two following close on. Everything is laid on in broad strokes. At the end of the first week, the director may (and often does) schedule run-throughs every day of the remaining weeks of rehearsals. A kind of benign bedlam sets in as the run-throughs stagger on without key cast members who have been pulled for costume fittings or music rehearsals. I mention this again to make it plain that what Mr. T. has been "freezing"—the staging of a piece of "business"—has practical value that presages what lies ahead for each of you. The more able you are to "take stage," the more valuable your performance will be to the musical—and to you. Most of the time you will be on your own when you are singing. Directors and choreographers may tell you what to do and where to go but how you execute these directions will depend on the degree of your expertise. It may be true that we are living in a time when musicals lean more heavily on their outer trimmings and trappings while their inner lives remain, for the most part, unattended to and empty. But great musicals do and have both. Stage yourself when you must, but then return and work out the life of the piece that gives meaning to its appearance. Do so and know that when it is finally on the stage, it will be of no great importance which came first.

Review

Miss W.'s and Mr. T.'s "Five" complete the technical work that has, until now, been our sole concern. Part Two, Performance, follows.

First, a summing-up:

1. *The "Five" must never be construed as a performance of the song.* It is a performance of a subtext—the "Two"—*on* a song; a subtext whose sole reason for being is to make the actor-singer physicalize every moment of the text. It must be apparent that this would be an insane thing to do when your only intention is to perform the song. In fact, there are many songs that gain their effect by less, rather than more, decoration. Why, then, the Five exercises?

a. The "One." We know now how much information is given to us by the lyricist. We know, too, the danger of making quick decisions about what a song "says"—decisions founded solely on our emotional response to the music of the song.

b. Do we do a "Two" on every song we sing? Of course not. As stated above, a "Two" is about moving all the time. Performing is about singing a song skillfully and intelligibly. When, then, a "Two?" Too often the actor-singer's range of physical expression is limited to empty gesturing. Now we know that when we *want* to move, we know *why* we move and *how* to move. It is not the words alone but the significance of what they are saying that informs a text with true and sane motor responses. At the same time, one does not need a "Two" to recognize that any great performance of a song knows what it is about, since *what it is about is why the song got to be sung in the first place.*

c. As I have said, there are many songs that will need little to no movement, so eloquent or complicated are their words. Nevertheless, we do not sing in a thoughtless vacuum any more than we speak in one. A "Two" is a stringing together of thought processes that result in body language. But all thought processes are not, by definition, "Twos." A single color word, a sudden revelation, a joke that is just around the corner and in need of "setting up"—none of these is a "Two" but each is incontestably a thought that as we have learned, will live in the "Air" between the lines (the "Three").

2. In my studio, when a performance lacks visual interest, I may suggest a "mini-Two." As an example: our old friend, Rodgers and

On Singing Onstage

Hart's "Where or When." The subject of dèjá vu is not without interest, but it does not impel the singer to move. To forestall standing always at "zero," and to make seeing the song as interesting as hearing it, it may be necessary to invent "frames" (physical action that frames the next line of the lyric) in the manner of a "Two":

> (*at "zero"*)
> It seems we stood and talked like this before,
> We looked at each other in the same way then,
> (*hands up from sides to "spike" the title*)
> But I can't remember where or when.
> (*hands together, as though chatting*)
> The clothes you're wearing are the clothes you wore,
> The smile you are smiling you were smiling then,
> (*resisting the urge to "do" nothing on the repeat line,*
> *hand to brow in confusion*)
> But I can't remember where or when.
> (*hands out in puzzled surrender*)
> Some things that happen for the first time
> Seem to be happening again.
> (*hands down and out for*)
> And so it seems that we have met before ... etc.

> ("Where or When," music and lyrics by Richard Rodgers and Lorenz Hart, from *Babes in Arms,* 1937. Copyright © 1937 by Chappell & Co., Inc. Copyright renewed. International copyright secured. All rights reserved. Used by permission.)

I hasten to acknowledge the infantilism of the above-suggested directions. They are used only as illustration and in no way are they intended to suggest a truly motivated performance of "Where or When."

3. Dialogue presents the actor with *heard* cues. Without them, he cannot react with his line. Monologues—and sung-monologues—are deprived of them. But speech, spoken or sung, still requires that thought give it its life. Where, then, can these thoughts (the *unheard* cues that constitute the subtext) be placed in order to justify the singing of each line, if not in the space (the "Air") that precedes it? If we accept this premise, we must acknowledge its conclusion:

> The actor-singer's *figurative script* is of his own making. It is *his* thinking that lives in the "Air" of the song. What we *hear* him sing is his reaction to this thought-flow—the *literal script* (the song) as it appears in the printed copy of the sheet music.

174

Great performing engages the eye as well as the ear. If we agree that each of us is unique, then our imprint on whatever we sing is uniquely our own. It is the singer who gives his songs their singularity. In the theater, the eye can fool the ear and steal the show. If your voice is less golden than your interpretive input, take heart.

PART TWO

Performance

16

Advice to the Songlorn

The point thereafter was to arrange for one's own chills and fever, passions and betrayals, chiefly in order to make song of them.

—James Merrill

HELD OPINIONS

One cannot codify the performance of songs the way we do the techniques that sustain those performances. Although there are many means to achieve even more ends, all judgments made of them are open to argument. I have tried to refrain from any discussion of which singer, what music, which style, or what sound is good, better, or best, since one man's preferred performer may very well leave another man cold. But although singing, no more or less than acting, cannot be reduced to rigid formulas, it is possible to set down, within strict margins, a definition of standards. These last chapters are an attempt to shed some light on the dark places that, in the beginning, can be so terrifying to the beginner actor-singer for whom the words of singing and music itself are alien. This is not to say that the singer cannot profit from the technical work in the preceding chapters, but the impressions and assessments that follow may run counter to those held by experienced professionals. None of them represents a hard and fast rule and all of them are personally held opinions. (For an in-depth study of the subject, I refer the reader to *On Performing,* McGraw-Hill Book Company, the companion volume to *On Singing Onstage.*)

The Coach or the Singing Teacher?

There is no question in my mind that the actor's and the dancer's terror of singing is due, in some part, to living in a world in which he never sings. The unknown can always be relied upon to provide a breeding ground for fear. I recommend an inexpensive antidote: Sing! Sing here, there, in the shower, at work, during a break, in the car—sing out! Get used to singing songs even if it strikes you as something less than making music. Don't let yourself be dissuaded by someone else's criticism of your vocal adequacy or in-. They probably don't sing any better than you do, and, if that is not enough to protect you against their thoughtlessness, cultivate a sense of humor about yourself, or, better still, sing when you are alone. But sing!

Where do you go from there? Two possible choices present themselves, both of which entail increased expense.

1. You can hire a pianist-cum-coach who will teach you some songs and accompany you when you stand in the bend of his piano and sing them. Or—

2. You can buy the services of a singing teacher and begin a serious study of the acoustical production of sound. (In whatever order you make these choices, I strongly advise getting around to the latter. Even if you never end up singing on a stage, you will have considerably improved your speaking voice.)

How do you choose either teacher? I suggest the time-honored method: Ask around. When you see someone who looks better than you do when he sings, or when you hear someone who sounds better than you do when he sings, find out the name of his coach or her singing teacher. Nothing and no one advertise teachers better than their students. Caveat One: Check out more than one recommendation. Teachers tend to exert a Svengali-like hold over their students. I have never heard anyone describe their singing teacher as anything less than brilliant. However, when you hear the same name over and over again, chances are that his reputation has been fairly earned. Caveat Two: Not every good singing teacher may turn out to be a good singing teacher for you. Since singing techniques are produced internally, a teacher cannot show you what to do so much as describe it. A verbal image may strike one man with clarity and leave another in confusion. Furthermore, there are many roads to Rome. The ideal one for you may call for further shopping around. If, after serious study, you have learned nothing, it would not be unreasonable to suppose that the fault is not all yours. But do not expect instant miracles. Discernible progress should be evident to both the teacher and the student after a period of around six months. (I have often heard professional singers claim a vocal technique that is a blend of more than one method, combined with an intimate awareness of the acoustical mechanism personal to their own bodies.)

Which experience should come first? It depends on you. If all you want to do is sing songs because you like to sing songs, or overcome the terror of singing songs, go with the coach. If you lean more toward a desire to know *how* to sing, the singing teacher will be your first choice. If you went with the coach, sooner or later you will find yourself asking, "Shouldn't I sing better?" If you chose the singing teacher you will inevitably wonder, "When do I get to sing something?"

The Accompanist—or Shoot the Pianist*

When the actor first begins to work with the coach of his choice he adopts an attitude of self-effacement and deference. The dancer and the singer are less enslaved because the pianist is an integral part of their daily lives. They and he live in a world of music—a world in which the actor is an immigrant all too willingly prepared to take orders. In the learning process this is as it should be. The coach may be coping with inadequacy on all counts. But when the actor-singer exits the studio and enters the theater—*his* domain—this complaisance can be self-annihilating. During a performance it must be the accompanist who registers a low profile. When he is more interesting than the performer, he is not doing his job according to the rules of the game. Worse, his preeminence over the proceedings places the unknowing performer in the absurd position of accompanying the accompanist.

Finally: We have talked of the danger of doing a singing audition accompanied by a pianist with whom you have never worked. It can now be seen that only a singer of experience and marked vocal refinement can disassociate himself from keyboard sound never heard before and

---

* (NOTE: The reverse of this exhortation is taken from Oscar Wilde's *Impressions of America: Leadville:* "Over the piano was printed a notice: 'Please do not shoot the pianist. He's doing his best.'")

musical fills that either enrapture or ravage the ear. I have never known a truly professional accompanist who prefers to annex territory that is not rightfully his. Ideally, he and the performer are fractions of the whole. When the singer needs more support it is forthcoming only to maintain the integer. Both are dedicated to the sublime act of making music. Remember: Performance on the stage is everything. No musical, no concert, no night-club act, and no TV variety program ever owed its success to an accompanist. I have *seen* songs sung by nonsinging performers that were memorable, and I have *heard* songs sung by singers that were stage-waits. In neither case were their accompaniments the root cause.

It is reasonable to confess you are a beginner when you first start to work with a coach. (It may be all too evident, but an early confession clears the air.) However, remember that you are buying his services, and, as in all commercial transactions, you will be paying for them. Be respectful, attentive, and eager to learn; be willing to fail and even find that amusing, but stay clear of excessive servility. If you surrender to it, along with his fee, you may have to pay dearly for it, too.

Three elements make up a singing experience:

1. choice of song;
2. quality of vocal presentation;
3. the performance as an entity, more commonly referred to as personal style.

Choice of Song

We have been choosing songs taken from one bin marked "What Not to Sing" (see Chapter Five, the "wrong song") and from another marked "Songs Better Left Unsung (see Chapter One: Words as Script). By now, your knowledge of what is dominant and recessive about you and your work should make easier your choice of the "right song" to sing. A coach can be of great help since he brings objectivity to the question of choice, as well as an encyclopedic knowledge of the available musical-theater repertory. With gained experience, the performer begins to sense when Song A is "just not for me" and be convinced, on sheer gut reaction, that Song B is "my song."

Once we have accepted the "right-or-wrong" theory, the choice of song is further defined by the circumstance of where it is to be sung. In a large night club? A small boîte? Does it open the act? Is it the peak of the act? The close of the act? A throwaway encore? Is it to be sung for

an audition for a musical? If so, how closely does it match the require-
ments of the score? And, within those limitations, how well does it advertise the singer's strong points and soft-pedal his weak ones? Given
the circumstances of where you sing it, even a right song may seem a
wrong choice.

Relative to choice: *You do not have to like the song you choose to
sing.* Just as an actor, having no particular fondness for a play, can play
it, the same can be said of the singer. We also falsely assume that our
affection for a song will engender the same response in the audience.
This is not necessarily so. There is even a point where liking a song too
much is dangerous in that it breeds an excess of "feelings." (Tyrone
Guthrie, the late and renowned English director, said to an actress:
"You're feeling it, you silly girl. Your job is to make *us* feel it.") The
bottom line: When a song you do not like gets you a job, it has a way
of becoming your special favorite.

Quality of Vocal Presentation

The musical theater has swung from one extreme—the sumptuous
vocal splendor of the imported Viennese and Gilbert and Sullivan op-
erettas of the late nineteenth century and the American imitations of the
same genre in the first decades of the twentieth century—to the opposite extreme wherein the works of Berlin, Rodgers and Hart, the
Gershwins, Porter, et al. stressed the performance of their material over
the quality of its sound. This is not to say that good singing went out of
fashion, only that the musical comedies that beguiled audiences in the
twenties, thirties, forties, and fifties contained scores that were not as
vocally demanding as the earlier product had been. In the sixties, rock-
oriented musicals called for yet another "sound" but this was a short-
lived phase. Now, in the last three decades of the twentieth century,
musical theater has reverted to scores that have to be sung. The singer
is back in fashion but more protean than before. She combines maximal
vocal range (e.g., *Evita*) with contemporary vocal mannerism (e.g., *Cats*
and *Les Miserables*) while, at the same time, sustaining dramatic tension
(e.g., all the work of Sondheim). Just as dancers learned to sing and to
act and demonstrated their ability to do all three so admirably in countless productions of *A Chorus Line*, singers are no longer the butts of
ridicule. The actor must begin to address the quality of his sound; to
train it to the maximum of its effectiveness.

Style

In *On Performing,* I wrote that "style" is a word that is not disposed kindly to definition. We use it to describe what is essentially inexplicable. We know for certain when a performer lacks it. We may even sense, when we see a performance, that it has it and we seem able to recognize its sum even when we have little or no idea what it is that constitutes the essential substance of its parts. Furthermore, style, like beauty, is very much in the eye of those who behold it. But on one thing we can all agree: When the quiddity of a performer is not there, style flies out the window, for it is only there to be seen when the essentiality of each of us is apparent.

We have previously identified the danger, when we sing, of abandoning ourselves to our feelings. A byproduct of the ability to mesh the "Two" to its related text in a "Three," a "Four," and a "Five" (see Chapters Thirteen, Fourteen, and Fifteen) is the growing awareness that thought and the "doing" of its business is as important to a song as our "feeling" it. Music, popular or serious, is a universal language. It induces inchoate feelings in an audience without any help from the singer. If he is not on guard, that potency of cheap music Mr. Coward spoke about is strong enough to melt the mind of the performer even as it melts the heart of the audience. The singer must begin to see himself not only as the creator of the vocal statement of the song, but the manipulator of the emotional responses of the audience to it. Who we *are* and what we *do* with the songs we sing teach our listeners not only to feel, but to feel as we do and as we wish them to. This power of the performer over his audience is the essence of his style.

Actors are renowned for playing parts. We say, "I *saw* him in *Hamlet,*" "I *saw* him play Lear." Singers reputations are built on: "I heard Billie *do* 'Strange Fruit,'" " ... Lena *do* 'Stormy Weather,'" " ... Judy *do* 'Over the Rainbow,'" " ... Sinatra *do* 'New York, New York.'" Even when we say an actor *did* a part, the timbre of the word is thinned. We do not say, "I saw Olivier do Vanya," but rather, "I saw Olivier's Vanya," because it implies that he *was* Vanya and not that he *did* him. But to say that I heard Jolson *do* "Swanee"—well, that says it all.

17

The Performance

First say to yourself what you would be, and then do what you have to do.

—Epictetus

MADE OBSERVATIONS

Performances are measured by those who witness them according to their own sights. It is not my intention here to move the reader away from credos born of the union of hard-earned experience and the sometimes crude realities of show-biz. There is no order to the observations I make on the disparate themes touched upon below. But, in total, they represent something of a credo of my own.

The Height of a Song

It is the importance—the interior height— of what you want to say that impels you to sing it instead. Songs live in the vertical. When the song you sing stays on the horizontal level, give it up and say it. Whenever a truly first-rate song is dead weight on the stage, it can be traced with certainty to a third-rate performance. The other side of this generalization: A brilliantly staged and performed third-rate song can stop a show cold in its tracks.

Every song contains within it its own elevation. You cannot stop its impulse to reach its maximum height. The best performer is not only aware of this arc and where its apogee occurs, but will be there moments before to make certain it gets there. A well-written song tends to hit its high point somewhere around the end of the Release (or Bridge) or somewhere within the last "8" of the Chorus. Rideouts may give the illusion that the song is soaring higher still, but they are not organic to the song's script. As described elsewhere, they are mechanical additions designed to hold on to the height claimed by the song and thereby induce applause.

I have said elsewhere that the singer, under all circumstances, must be more interesting than the songs he sings. If every song can be said to possess its own height, it is imperative that the wise performer choose to sing songs less tall than he. "Rose's Turn," from *Gypsy*, an Everest in the repertory of theater music, would not be ideal audition material. Even the late Ethel Merman, a Watusi among singing artists, was able to hold sway over its power only by virtue of having played her way through the entire score and libretto. Furthermore, its references lose their pertinence when the song is taken out of context. The songs you sing in the body of your audition should not require verbal settings to render them understandable to the listener.

It is in the Vamp of the song you sing that its vertical journey begins. Two thought processes are recommended to help you move from neutral to high gear.

1. When you come center in the Vamp, an imperative demand for attention can be made by inserting the cue "Listen to me!" Once established, don't permit it to thin down to "Listen to me, please." This is an order you are giving and not a favor being asked.

2. More light in weight but no less urgent is the old chestnut: "I have a great song to sing for you!" It can be changed to "I have a great sad song to sing for you!" ... or " ... a great swinging song to sing for you!" but, in all cases, the pivotal words will always be " ... for you!"

Both sentences demand attention. Once gained, be sure delivery is made. Promise what you know to be forthcoming—and keep your promise.

Since there is no hiding place in the songs you sing, always be sure it is *you* singing them. Don't invent anyone to sing them for you. (The exception would be an audition for which you are asked to prepare a specific characterization unlike the *you* that presents itself when you enter onto the stage.) If it is acceptable that nothing you will ever sing will be more important than you singing it, remember that even those pivotal words " ... for you!" valuable as they may be, are not as imposing as the word "I ... " that begins the sentence.

Of all the roads that lead to personal defeat, none is more apt to erase the sight and sound of you from the consciousness of the auditioner than singing a song with only its words and music on your mind. I do not mean to imply that beauty, grace, and a ravishing voice are not, in themselves, preemptively interesting. But the lack of them need not be inimical to what is recognized as stageworthy. I have seen great performances barely sung (Walter Huston vocalizing "September Song," the Kurt Weill–Maxwell Anderson standard from *Knickerbocker Holiday*) and I have heard memorable singing come from out of the mouths of less than beautiful faces (the unforgettable Piaf and Libby Holman). In performance the power these performers exerted over their material, whether personal or vocal, made them great singers and, in the truest meaning of the word, great beauties.

There are many "scripts" that can be said to mastermind your thinking, but only one guarantees your personal signature on everything you sing: Trust that who and what you are, by virtue of their uniqueness, are worthy of being attended. Demand and hold attention by staying in the *now* of the song and proceed, in its vocalization, from moment to moment. Convey the impression that, although it is *your* song, you do not know what you are going to say or even where it may lead—at the same time that you know all to well where you are, where you are going, and, most important of all, where you must be before you get there. And, finally, know where the dramatic intensity in the lyric heightens and know those places so well that your *build to them is why they occur.*

A well-written song helps you to accomplish these ends by gaining interest as it proceeds, the second "8" being more interesting than the first, the Bridge or Release even more so, but less so than the last "8." All of this is elemental to the art of good lyric writing. The energy of your thinking should keep pace with this growing tension. An example of this is the performance of Rex Harrison singing "I've Grown Accustomed to Her Face" in the film of *My Fair Lady*. Instead of information delivered (the lyric can be trusted to do that if it is well articulated), we see the misogynist Higgins enduring the anguish of the revelation of dependency upon Eliza Doolittle who, but a moment before, he protested was but "an owl sickened by a few days of my sunshine! Very well! Let her go! I can do without her! I can do without anybody! I have my own soul! My own spark of divine fire!" This pain is not realized until he runs out of bluster and then we see a defeated man surrendering to the first passion of his life at the very same moment that we hear a lovely ballad. Beautiful as the song incontestably is, it cannot take our attention away from Higgins/Harrison. Here, then, is a perfect example of a great song sung more greatly still.

You may "do" a song in any way you choose as long as it does not do the song in. Even this warning can be disregarded if it is seen to work. Sometimes I am caught up by the daring of a singer and realize, yet again, that every song is new when newly sung. Not to resist the pun, I once watched Tony Newley sing Cole Porter's "It's All Right With Me" from *Can-Can*. He posed himself, for no apparent reason, as Rodin's "The Thinker" and managed to keep everyone's attention riveted on both him and the song. Would I or you have chosen to sing it thus? No. Do I even suggest that it is an ideal or even a justifiable interpretation of the text? No. But I would not deny that, for the three or four minutes he held sway, so did the song.

Provocative and oppositional choices may have merit, and this is especially true in comic material where the temptation to be and to "do" funny can be counterproductive. In an interview with Philip Roth after the publication of his novella *The Breast*, in which a man literally transmutes into the book's title, Mr. Roth said his goal was " ... to resist exploiting an idea in large part because the possibility is so apparent. It strikes me that what is most obvious is thus the least promising way of treating a character in a situation. If the joke was there before I even began, I thought perhaps the best thing was to stand it on its head by refusing to take it as a joke."

Oppositional choices may be applied to a musical arrangement by going counter to the scoring of the song, although I would not suggest singing it for the composer, who may not find the conceit as amusing as you do. For example: Streisand's dirgelike reading of the up-tempo "Happy Days Are Here Again." In my studio, I have often up-tempo'd ballads to gain similar and striking results. Two examples of the slow-to-fast conversion: Rodgers and Hammerstein's "All at Once You Love Her" from *Pipe Dream* and Cole Porter's "I Am Loved" from *Out of This World*.

If it is true that you may do a song in almost any way you choose, it is equally true that you should resist doing it in any way that will do you in. Chief among those "handles":

1. Loser songs sung by losers. In my experience I have not met the

director or the hirer at a musical audition who can distinguish between a loser and someone playing the part. Tell them out front that you are a failure and you will never brook an argument. Resistance to this warning can be tempting when you realize how many wonderful standard show tunes are out there waiting to shipwreck you—for example, Rodgers and Hart's "Little Girl Blue," Kern and Hammerstein's "Why Was I Born?" the Gershwin Brothers "But Not for Me," Dietz and Schwartz's "By Myself," Arlen and Gershwin's "The Man That Got Away" … and on into infinitum. Of course, *this does not mean that these songs are not to be sung. Only that they are not to be loser-sung.*

2. Shun self-pity, the pitiful, and the pitiable. What may score for the Little Match Girl on a wintry street corner has the opposite effect on an audience who has already paid the price of admission. Blues songs are particularly vulnerable to this approach. Again, they are not denied you, but wit and positive thinking will do more for you than all the blue lights thrown on all the blue ladies and gentlemen stuck with and in the blues.

Performance vs. Staging

There is a distinct difference between these two words. As I have defined it, the *performance* of a song is born in the instant, with each instant birthing new objective and subjective revelations. On the other hand, choreographers *stage* songs, less often in solo than in production numbers because, without prescribed movement patterns, anarchy would result. It is the "doing" rather than an organic "experiencing" of the song that characterizes *staging*. Uniformity is rigidly attended to and its execution is always by the numbers and "on the beat." The choreographer, when he doubles as the director, may stage a soloist ("I want you to do *this* here and do *this* here and, in the second "8," cross and do *this* here). His classic defense: "If I don't tell him what to do, he won't do anything." Nothing testifies to the diminishing ability of today's performers more than this dependency on instruction on how to "take stage."

In an audition of your work, staging yourself by "freezing" what you do can have a reverse effect. What was seen to be pleasing to the eye in a performance of the song within the context of the musical now muddles and hides the one element that should take precedence over everything—you. I confess to a certain sadness when I see a performer stage his life in a song (as a hedge against failure) when, under the rules of an audition, the very act of self-concealment defines a failed audition. If freeze you must, freeze your *thinking,* and the "doing" of the song will take care of itself. Better to do nothing than to present a carbon copy of yourself each time you show your work. At the very worst, *nothing* leaves open to question whether, if you had wished to, you would have done *something.*

OFFERED SUGGESTIONS

Held opinions softened to made observations. Now they give way to offered suggestions in which the author's personal taste is less disguised.

Movement

How much physical statement does a song need to gain its effect? Unlike the depth of the ocean and the height of the sky, there are definable limits we can set for ourselves.

An audience, given the option to look or to listen, can always be expected to watch what is going on. A parochial glossary of one-liners testifies to an ancient theater language that has been with us since the early Greeks and probably long before then, when it was found that a grunt was less interesting than the hopping up and down that accompanied it. "Would you please stand still! I'm telling a joke here!" "Would you please move down? I don't know what it is you're doing up there but whatever it is, stop it!" "I hope he isn't planning to make that entrance on my line?!" "Do you have to light that cigarette just then?" These are all lines an actor can be expected to whine, complain, or mutter at least once in his career and, at most, once during every appearance he will make.

It must be obvious, even to the rankest beginner, that what a song says and how it chooses to say it should determine the extent of allowable movement. The speed of the delivery of the complicated rhyme structures of many of Sondheim's more extravagant songs, Rodgers and Hart's "I Wish I Were in Love Again," Gilbert and Sullivan's tongue-twisters—these songs require absolute attention if the audience is to get the gist and the joke. Anything busier than minimal movement would be counterproductive to both the author's and the performer's intentions. In addition, when complex writing is replaced by dense emotion, there is the same need to remain simple: Lerner and Loewe's "I Still See Elisa" from *Paint Your Wagon* is sung by an old man whose love for a long-dead wife is still very much alive. The song, a slow valse triste, is at its most affecting when its delivery is unembellished. At the other extreme are the songs that say little to nothing and allow the performer all the room he needs to make them work. In Chapter Four: The Audition, I wrote that "I'm Gonna Wash That Man Right Outa My Hair" is nothing but an accompaniment to a shampoo. As such, it is a perfect song. Its melody and text are mere musical sounds that in no way would intrude upon the delight of an audience watching Nellie wash her hair.

These extremes are the outer limits of a vast library of vocal music in which some kind of movement can be expected to enhance performance. Generally speaking, straight ballads call for less decoration than "large" songs. "Memories," for example, does not ask for the sized physical life that "Don't Rain on My Parade" demands. "Over the Rainbow" can be sung standing quite still with little to no physical framing, whereas "Gimme a Pigfoot and a Bottle of Beer" asks that you move when you sing it or you cannot be said to *be* singing it. The movement inherent in rock and roll is so natural a part of its life that if it doesn't come to you instinctively, you should not be singing it at all.

For those who can dance, there are songs whose titles sing for themselves: "I've Got Shoes with Wings On," "Pick Yourself Up," "I Want to Be a Dancing Man," "I Can Do That," and "I Won't Dance," along with songs whose original presentation is associated with a dancer: "All I Need Is the Girl," "The Music and the Mirror," "The Lullaby of Broadway." The vocalization of these songs need not be danced as they are sung—in fact, the first makes the second almost impossible—but eight or sixteen bars of a second chorus in which the dancer shows his colors is a worthwhile addition to his audition repertory. (I recommend the films of Fred Astaire to study how simply the master sang his songs before he "took off" and danced them.) For those who sing so that they can dance and then follow it with a chorus that puts the lie to the lyric, I suggest they abandon the suicide, return to their dance studies, perfect their time steps, and belly up to the barre.

Hands

1. When you first begin to layer body language onto a song, a good rule to follow: Inhibit the *high* and *wide* of your hands by constructing imaginary walls and ceilings beyond and above which they are not permitted to go. In the beginning, the narrower the walls and the lower the ceilings, the better. Once you are in control of them, you can always allow them further liberties.

2. Resist symmetry when you can. Too much of one hand doing what the other is doing can have a tedious and tranquilizing effect on the eye. Train yourself to work, on occasion, with hands in opposition to each other even if, in the beginning, it seems arbitrary and mechanical.

3. Hands can be used to *spike* a line; to point up a joke; to frame a title the first time it is heard (see below). Remember that this "punctuation" is subject to the same rules that apply to all physical movement: It should *precede* and not smear over and through the line (see Chapter Thirteen: The "Three").

4. Just as it is important to "frame" a title the first time the audience hears it, so that they can more readily *see* it, it is ill-advised to give it any further importance each time the title reappears. All subsequent reprises of the title should be treated just as you would any repeat line. Move all over them. The reverse of the above-stated rule: When there is nothing to listen to, give the audience something to look at. If a repeat line can be described as a mini-stage-wait, perhaps a mini-"Two"?

Once I laughed when I heard you saying
That I'd be playing solitaire,
Uneasy in my easy chair
(*hands out to frame title 1*)
It never entered my mind.
Once you told me I was mistaken,
That I'd awaken with the sun
And order orange juice for one.
(*"What a laugh! It was absolutely out of the question!"*)
It never entered my mind.
You have what I lack myself,
And now I even have to scratch my back myself.
Once you warned me that if you scorned me
I'd sing the maiden's pray'r again
And wish that you were there again
To get into my hair again.
(*"My God! How far I've come!"*)
It never entered my mind.

5. I have always believed that one reason the beginner performer finds so little comfort in standing alone on stage and singing out is because the increase in his visibility engenders a concurrent sensation that a shared sexual experience is part of this new game—an experience he had not bargained for but one he must take into account. Whereas the actor is dressed in the role he plays and the dancer's art apotheosizes rather than arouses, the singer is up there, on his own, all alone and only too aware that he is the single focus of the audience's attention and examination: the object of their sexual fantasies. One has only to recall the effect of a Sinatra on the teenage audiences of his time and Elvis Presley's and the Beatles' impact on their fans to understand how intimate is the relation between the singer and his songs, and those to whom he sings them. We watch a singer in his wholeness; his very physical appearance is there for our delight; he is available, open, giving. Even the subject matter and its musical arrangement is shaped to awaken emotional responses that are personal to each listener in the audience. Of course, bad performing stays far away from the bedroom of our minds but great performers are like great lovers. Rather than resisting the role, they lead, direct, and manipulate our reactions in ways so subtle we may not even be aware of the tactics they employ. A most simple illustration:

Hands are at "zero" when they are at our sides. In this position, the body language has literally nothing to say. Held low in front of us or clasped behind our backs, they can still be described as being at "zero," but a subtle shading has come into play. By holding our hands in front of us, small talk or innocent conversation is implied: The simple expedient of covering up the lower part of the body appears to dictate the allowable aspect of intimacy. The opposite effect is gained by clasping hands behind the back. In this "zero," the performer presents a full-length view of the body that seems to invite total scrutiny. I repeat: All three hand positions can be said to be at "zero," but they have gone from "zero" to "zero plus" to "plus zero" with increasing intimacy. This order can be used to good effect in verses that begin with straight exposition, move into more specific language, and end in the personal references that set up the chorus.

It can be said, then, that hands conceal as well as reveal. In my teaching, I take issue with movement for movement's sake unless the style of the performer and his personal way of moving is so unique as to give meaning even to meaninglessness. Excess of anything is counterproductive. It is said that William Macready, the great nineteenth-century English tragedian, concerned about a tendency toward overgesturing, would bind his body in strings of worsted. When a string broke, he would know for certain that the move was essential to his performance. This may be too much of a good thing. I would suggest a simpler system: When, at any moment in your performance, you become aware of what you are physically "doing," consider whether or not, if you excised it, it would be missed.

Of this you can be sure: once you commit the words and music of a song to memory, your mouth will not let you down. It will keep singing out that song even if all you have on your mind is your laundry list. But your hands and feet can always be trusted to tell the truth. With only that laundry list to cue them, they will go their own insane way. In that sense, they are the great betrayers.

Feet

1. Where you want to stand when you sing on a stage is that ideal geography: downstage center. Need you remain there? No. Songs begin there and major lines in the lyric belong there, but when the length of a song allows it, your feet can take you Left or Right of Center, as long as you make the trip worth the taking. (Moving down is denied you for you are, or should be, already standing in the furthermost downstage position.) Lateral moves can give variety to songs that tend to pall if they stay too long in Center. However, when you find you are singing in the unflattering glow of a work light whose amperage would leave you in semidarkness if you ventured too far to the Left or Right, restraint is recommended. But in a white room or on a fully lighted stage, it would be to your advantage to travel and "work" the stage. One precautionary note: End the song back where you started, in Center. Rideouts are weakened when they are played out on first or third base.

2. Upstage moves are to be shunned since they diminish the size of the performer by lengthening the trajectory of the eye. But if you feel there is good reason to move "up," increase the importance of your thinking and the physical language it manifests. You will then be seen to have balanced out the gain in distance with an increase in the sight and size of you.

Your overriding impulse will always be to service the song; to make it more interesting to listen to (how well you sing it) and to watch (how well you perform it). How decoratively you choose to move in your performance of the song is a matter of choice which, in turn, is decreed by the nature of the material. If your intention remains consistently clear, you can move up, you can go Right and you can go Left—but you will never go wrong.

Don'ts

What we are we know we are. What we look like to others we are destined never to know with certainty. Although any one of the following *Don'ts* may not seem, from the inside, to be working against the sight of you, each is less than valuable when seen from the outside:

1. Stay away from physical indications of the pronouns *I, me,* and *you*. What you are saying rarely depends on pointing out who you, he, she, or they are.

2. Stay away from the flashing smile that accompanies, in mindless partnership, the words *happy, glad, pleased, joy(ous), merry, cheery,* and all their synonyms. I sometimes go so far as to play the reverse of what I say, e.g.:

> Like a straying baby lamb
> With no mammy and no pappy,
> I'm so (*an ironic smile*) unhappy,
> But oh, so (*slow transition to misery*) glad.

> ("Glad to Be Unhappy," music and lyrics by Richard Rodgers and Lorenz Hart, from *On Your Toes*, 1936. Copyright © 1936 by Chappell & Co., Inc. Copyright renewed. International copyright secured. All rights reserved. Used by permission.)

3. Stay away from the shrug. If body language can be said to speak your thoughts, a shrug implies indifference. "Who cares?" may very well be read, by the audience, as the singer's suggested response to his performance.

Props

If the lyrics of a song are its text, and what we choose as their significance its subtext, then the proper handling of a prop, while we sing, must be assigned a third script. Given its head, a prop will happily take over the proceedings until you and your song are barely visible. Years ago I heard a story ascribed to the eminent actor Joseph Schildkraut, who recalled an incident that occurred when he was a boy away at school in Austria. With each appearance he made in a school play, he would beseech his father by letter to come to see him act. The father,

On Singing Onstage

Maurice Schildkraut, was an actor of great renown with no interest whatever in children, kin or no, on a stage. But at last the old man agreed, out of conscience or curiosity, to attend a performance of *King Lear* in which his son, no more than fifteen at the time, was to appear in the leading role. The sight of the boy in a grey wig and penciled-in winkles must have caused him great pain. Finally, unable to watch his son stroking a hooked-on long white beard, he rose from his seat, raised his arms and eyes heavenward, and cried out, "Beard! Where are you going with my son!?"

The story has been told and retold, and for all I know it may be more fiction than fact, but it serves to illustrate the point: Subjugate and enslave a prop or it very soon becomes your master. Do you want to take out a cigarette, strike a match, light the cigarette, inhale and exhale the smoke ... and do it all while you sing your song? The idea reads a good deal more easily than it performs. Do you want to take off your glasses, play with them, pocket them, take them out again, and put them back on? Do you want to work a jacket? Get in or out of a coat? All valid props with appropriate activities assigned to them. But they are all a busy-ness until they work from a "third script" whose sole purpose is to manipulate them in the same way that a subtext works—to the advantage of the song. Just as ignorance of a prop's power can be expected to upstage the amateur, knowledge of how to work it proclaims the professional.

I recall a performance of Rodgers and Hart's "Did You Ever Get Stung?" by a celebrated actress in the theater who constructed it in my studio as an exercise in prop work. She put on and adjusted furs, and, in the second "8," took out a compact and a lipstick from her bag and freshened her makeup. The powdering of her nose, carefully placed in spaces of the lyric that permitted it, was reserved for the Bridge:

Did you say, "She lives for me!
This is it! Now at last!"
You bit! You were it!
You got hit by the blast!

We placed a rim-shot after the last word, and, to punctuate it, she closed the compact with a snap that released a puff of powder around her face that framed the word *blast* with a mini-explosion. The last "8" and the Rideout extension were filled out with putting on her gloves, timed so that the last finger was in place on the last beat of the Rideout. She was ready and set to leave and leave she did. The performance became the kingpin of her audition material, but I doubt if those who applauded it ever realized the work that went into the timing of the "business" assigned to each prop (the third script) that, in turn, set off the subtext (the second script) that triggered the lyric (the first script) and made the performance seem an effortless setting for Rodgers and Hart's charming 2/4 tune.

When a prop appears out of nowhere, and, for no reason other than the whim of the performer, lives for a moment and then hangs around with nothing to do but grow like young Schildkraut's beard—strike it. There are those, like the late Danny Kaye, who are blessed with a talent for "working" props and there are otherwise splendid artists who have neither the facility nor the imagination to carry them off. It is, after all, a very special gift, but those who lack it need not feel a sense of great loss. Memorable performances are played out in an infinite variety of languages. Props are only one idiom. An afterthought: The appliquéing of props onto a song, no matter how skillfully worked, has a tendency to pall when it stays on stage too long. Like a trick well done, once it has accomplished its task and gained its effect, it is over and done.

Focus

In Chapter One, an *objective* lyric was identified by the presence of the word *you* in its text. In Chapter Nine, a Center spot was reserved for that *you* as the exclusive focus to whom the performer worked. For example, in "Send in the Clowns," from its very beginning, " ... me here at last on the ground, you in mid-air" straight through to the finish of the song, " ... well, maybe next year," the *me* (the singer of the song) and the *you* remain constant. The song belongs to the explicit *you*, and its life is lived in the Center focus. A change in focus that is not substantiated in the lyric would confuse the audience.

However, when the explicit *you* implies *you-all*, the song is characterized as a "house number," e.g., "If You Feel Like Singing, Sing!" "Forget your troubles and just Get Happy! You better chase all your blues away!" and "When it all comes true, just the way you planned, it's funny but the bells don't ring—it's A Quiet Thing." To play a house number to an exclusive center focus would be both confining and restrictive since, by definition, it belongs to everyone. In the *technical* work on focus in Chapter Nine, you worked to three, and only three spots: Center, Left, and Right. In the *performance* of a house number, *you are free to play to any and every part of the theater or room.*

The following ground rules may keep unrestrained freedom from turning into chaos. To begin with, work the first line of the lyric to a general focus. This announces, right at the start, that the song is meant for everyone. Imagine, as you "pan" the audience, that you are talking to a group of people and not to any one person in particular. If the lyric permits, a second line may be similarly played, but I would not risk more than two lines to the theater at large, at peril of turning the song into a speech. As noted elsewhere, a good lyric has an innate "build" written into it. First (and possibly second) lines, played to a general focus, set the circumstances; second (or third) lines, played to lateral spots, tend to be setups for the final "pay-off" or punch line—always directed to the center for maximum effect. This is, of course, rank generalization, but the Porter Verse to our old favorite, "Make It Another Old-Fashioned, Please," will help to illustrate the point:

(*General focus*)
Since I went on the wagon, I'm
Certain drink is a major crime,
(*Left focus*)
For when you lay off the liquor
(*Right focus*)
You feel so much slicker,
(*Center*)
Well, that is, most of the time.

What will always rule your choice of focus will be the significant weight of what you are *going to say.* As a rule worth following, you can never go too wrong by giving to Center important lines in the lyric: the first mention of the title of the song, a joke, the top of a Bridge, and the last line (more often than not) of the lyric. These are all power lines that may be weakened when they are not highly visible to the house. For "highly visible," read Center. Once you have laid them in, the rest of the script may be directed either generally or laterally, as you see fit.

An impulse to make what you are singing *important* may result in "pushing against the fourth wall." The performer, intent upon giving urgency to what he is singing, presses on the spot, and, by so doing, invites the opposite reaction—the more pressure, the more I suspect nothing is there. Let us agree that the theater (the audience, the auditioner, and the spot[s] you sing to) *is* there. Insisting that it is there will not make it *more* there. What gives focus credibility is its effect on you. I believe there is a life out front to the degree that I read its presence on you. If you see it, you will react to it. You do not have to *do* you seeing it. Staring down a focus to give proof of its reality will only give the lie to it.

Finally, I have noticed that once the beginner is introduced to focus as a cure for the disease of rolling eyeballs, he embraces a Center focus with unswerving allegiance. Remember: Unless the lyric expressly speaks to one person (the explicit *you* we have spoken about), songs belong to everyone. Why force them to live in a prison when they are free to go where they please? Yes, there is safety in latching onto one spot and never deviating from the security of its lifeline. But there is greater joy in risking singing out for the sheer pleasure of making music and, more to the point, sharing that pleasure with those for whom your songs are intended.

Learning a Song

When you learn the words and music of a song, it may be said that you know it. But it is quite another ball game when you know how to perform it, to make it work for you on a stage. As you have seen in the technique sections of this volume, a performance, to continue the metaphor, cannot be said to have left the dugout unless you have:

1. phrased it to make the lyric intelligible, and to enable you to sing it high, low, and well;

2. decided on the significance of the text and constructed the flow of interior cues that stamp the song as your own;

3. made focus choices;

4. elected where you will move, if at all, and timed your physical life to frame what you are going to say, and, lastly;

5. learned to live comfortably in the "Air" in the music, and to make it appear that the long or short of it was not the composer's choice but your own.

It is not necessary to carry around an attaché case crammed with audition material. Five or six well-chosen songs are more than enough to service you. If you are a singer, they should include proof of your ability to make music; if you dance, have one or two numbers that, in Agnes de Mille's perfect phrase, "take the air"; if your talent to amuse is your calling card, be prepared to advertise it; and if you are an actor who can sing, include at least one song in which your interpretive talent takes precedence over possible vocal inadequacy. I have written at great length on this subject in a companion volume, *On Performing*. The point to be made here is to underline the importance of performing a few songs well, rather than knowing the words and music of dozens of them, none of which you do at all.

WORDS WORDS WORDS

The Poetic Lyric

There are simple lyrics, complicated lyrics, dramatic lyrics, heart-breaking lyrics. There are tricky lyrics, profound lyrics, lyrics that tell stories, and lyrics that say nothing. But of all the words written to be sung, none is more difficult to give life to than the "poetic" lyric. For example:

Out of my dreams and into your arms
I long to fly.
I will come as evening comes
To woo a waiting sigh.
Out of my dreams and into the hush
Of falling shadows,
When the mist is low,
And stars are breaking through,
Then out of my dreams I'll go,
Into a dream with you.

> ("Out of My Dreams," music and lyrics by Richard Rodgers and Oscar Hammerstein II, from *Oklahoma!*, 1943. Copyright © 1943 by Williamson Music, Inc. Copyright renewed. International copyright secured. All rights reserved. Used by permission.)

If this beautiful lyric and the lovely waltz Mr. Rodgers assigned to it are all you have on your mind when you sing it, there is a good chance that you will not know who you are, why you are singing it, what you are talking about, and why, as you work your way through it, you begin to feel like a column of cement. Poetic lyrics may sound alluring but they are far removed from the language we speak and farther still from the small-talk images we create to feed the word flow. Here are two defenses that will defuse their destructive power.

1. In the preparation (only) of the performance, be sure you translate the words. Know what you are saying—and make certain your translation is in plain English.

2. Keep your subtext, no matter how important, in the vernacular. You cannot restrain the sung lyric from soaring, but you can refrain from flying with it by keeping your *thinking* language on the ground.

Diction

1. Lyrics written for the musical theater tend to be more literary than their "pop" counterparts. Gershwin, Hart, Lerner, Fields, Sondheim, Ebb, Dietz, and Harnick, among others, were and are masters of light verse. Each of us knows how infuriating it can be when what we hear is audible (PA systems take care of that), but not understandable. As your way with a song becomes easier, resist easy articulation. What you may think is too much may, for those out front, be just enough. This is not a chat you are having but a song you are singing. Its speech is governed by the laws of prosody; it is rhymed, lean, and often dense. As part of a score, it is created to move a story, illuminate character, or pass on important information. In the hands of a first-class lyricist, it may do all three. It is worth remembering that "What did he say/sing?" murmured too often, yields to "I don't give a damn."

2. When you sing, it is the vowel that makes music of the words. But the consonants that surround it make the word. After a held vowel, remember that you have not finished the word until its final consonant is attended to. As a safeguard, explode it.

Phrases Within Phrases

1. Rather than thinking of the verbal line as one nonstop flow of words, sharpen your awareness of the elements within a sentence that give it special meaning. Phrasing from lyric (see Chapter Three) can help spotlight what otherwise might be lost. For example, the last "8" of Ogden Nash's "Roundabout":

Then it's roundabout and roundabout
And roundabout once more (✔)
As you pray again
Each day again to soar (*no breath*)
On your way (,—*glottal stop*) again (✔)
It's roundabout once more.

2. Spotlight qualifying words and descriptives that give a line its unique tone—as in Oscar Hammerstein's

When the sky is a bright *canary* yellow.

3. If there is a twist to a lyric, help to give it prominence. If it can be said that a great performer makes his songs his own, here is one, by Lorenz Hart, to be proud of.

You are so fair,
Like an oriental vision,
But you won't make that decision.
You're not quite fair.
I'd pay your fare
To Niag'ra Falls and back, too,
But you never will react to
This love affair.
You are the crepes suzette
I should get on my bill of fare,
But if you love me not,
Flower-pot,
See if I care!
See how you'll fare
If you keep on playing rover
When I come to think it over,
You're only fair.

("You Are So Fair," music and lyrics by Richard Rodgers and Lorenz Hart, from *Babes in Arms*, 1937. Copyright © 1951 by Chappell & Co., Inc. International copyright secured. All rights reserved. Used by permission.)

This homonymnal hymn has a last-line twist that not only takes back the all-out rave of the first line, but turns the homophone into a homograph.

Phrasing Postscripts—Random *Don'ts* and *Do's*

1. When two explosive consonants (e.g., b, d, f, k, p, t) follow each other—hub-bub, dead drunk, life force, black coal, pip-pip, and the two examples below:

Thou noble, upright, truthful, sincere
And slightly dopey gent

and

> There'll be a hot time in the old town tonight

—it is only necessary to explode the second consonant, namely the "t" of "truthful" and the "t" of "time." If, however, in the first instance, you choose to take a beat between "upright" and "truthful," the rule would not hold. But if the adjectives are run together in an avalanche of affection for the chap, the second "t" will do admirable double duty. I can think of no exception to the second instance. A "hot time" for a singer, in the vocal sense, will be a "hah time" and thereby eliminate the stuttered t's—or better still, the stutter(∅) t's.

2. In Chapter Three: Phrasing, I wrote that when you need a breath, " ... breathe where the least damage will be done to the text. More often than not, this will be least noticeable before articles, conjunctions and/or prepositions." This rule has one exception: When the verb includes a preposition—e.g., tell to, work in, work at or work for, sing to, and cry about—do not separate the verb from its preposition and, instead, grab your breath as soon after as possible.

3. In the theater, it is a rare rule that has no exceptions, but here for the singing performer, is one worth consideration: When you take a breath at the end of a line to gain sufficient air to continue singing, always breathe at the expense of *what you have just said* and never at the expense of *what you are going to say*. Better to cut off that extra minisecond from the already-sung last word than to rob precious minimoments from the first words you are about to sing. Audiences are less aware of what they missed than of what they are missing. Even more important, you will have the gratitude of the conductor/accompanist. Downbeats, along with the tides and time, wait for no man.

Bad English—Good Lyrics

1. In every language, there are words that, when they are elided, mean something quite different from when they are separate and apart. Unelide them. Without further explanation, the following examples should make the point clear:

"And the world discovers as my book (,) ends ... "
the vulgarism:

"It's (,) not where you start but where you finish"
the scatological:

"Isn't (,) it romantic?"

and,

"Her (,) ears are extraordinary ears"
and the topper:
"I'm wearing my heart (,) on my sleeve"
   2. Lyrics, when they are read, often look like extracts from a Latin
pony ("throw the horse over the fence some oats"). Good syntax will
always lose out to rhyme:

You've got what Adam had
When he with love for Eve was tortured,
She only had an apple tree
But you, you've got an orchard!

   ("You've Got That Thing," music and lyrics by Cole Porter, from *Fifty Million
   Frenchmen*, 1929. Copyright © 1929 Warner Bros., Inc. Copyright renewed.
   All rights reserved. Used by permission.)

And although we *say*: "Someday the man I love will come along" and
"And so, above all else, I'm waiting for the man I love," we *sing*:

Someday he'll come along,
The man I love

and:

And so all else above,
I'm waiting for the man I love.

   ("The Man I Love," music and lyrics by George and Ira Gershwin, from *Lady
   Be Good*, 1924.)

But what reads awkwardly will sing with no loss of grace. "The Man I
Love" presents further justification for the need to *think ahead*. If " ... the
man I love" is not on your mind when you are singing " ... someday he'll
come along," your reading of the first line, for all the audience knows,
may refer to the Grim Reaper or a visitor from the IRS.

The Dying Fall

   Without risking argument, there is one aspect of spoken American
speech that distinguishes us from our English cousins: The dying fall.
Read that sentence out loud and it will be clear to you that almost
everything we say is a tonal downer. This predisposition to drop the

melody and energy of what we say works against us when speech is sung. A well-written lyric builds to the end of the phrase. Begin to train yourself to hear language in a new way; as the line moves toward its resolution, consciously increase the dynamic of your thinking and the energy level of your vocal projection. Resist the dying fall by singing the line with this intention:⁀ rather than ⁀ . You will be pleased to hear how you improved the line reading and often to serendipitous advantage. I have heard Irving Berlin's "Change Partners" innumerable times. The first "8" is always sung with the last verb accented:

> Must you dance every dance
> With the same fortunate man?
> You have danced with him since the music began
> Won't you change partners and *dance* with me?

> ("Change Partners," music and lyrics by Irving Berlin, from the film *Carefree*, 1938. Copyright © 1937, 1938 by Irving Berlin. Copyright renewed 1964, 1965 by Irving Berlin. Reprinted by permission of Irving Berlin Music Corporation.)

But not out of the mouth of Fred Astaire. He resists the dying fall by singing " ... won't you change partners and dance with *me?*" suggesting that *dancing* is not the issue but rather *with whom*. When the melodic line rises at its end, the dying fall is averted. And sometimes the composer scores the money word on a vocal rise in order to strengthen and insure its audability, e.g., the penultimate line of the last "8" of Gershwin's "I Got Rhythm":

> I got rhythm,
> I got music,
> I got my man—
> Who could ask for anything more?
> Who could ask for anything more?

> ("I Got Rhythm," by George and Ira Gershwin, from *Girl Crazy*, 1930. Copyright © 1930 New World Music Corporation. Copyright renewed. All rights reserved. Used by permission.)

but the first "8" needs the singer's help to defy the dying fall.

The Weak and the Strong

In every bar of music, there are strong and weak rhythmic accents.

In a march (4/4 time), the first and third beats are strong; the second and fourth beats are weak, e.g.:

LEFT, right, LEFT, right, etc.

In a waltz (3/4 time), the first beat is strong; the second and third beats are weak, e.g.:

OOM pah pah, OOM pah pah, etc.

When a money word that has substantive importance falls on an *unaccented* beat, the singer has to "white light" it or it will disappear with no trace. In our anthem, the line " ... whose broad stripes and bright stars" crams " ... whose broad" into the upbeat that precedes "stripes" on the downbeat. Giving "broad" its due is almost impossible. Most of us settle for:

whose braw stripes, etc.

This condition occurs more often than you may imagine. Remember: There is no need to single out the word "stripes." It inherits the energy implicit in the downbeat. But to bring "whose *broad*" to the fore takes some doing.

Held opinions, made observations, and offered suggestions—all subjective by virtue of the inexactitude of art—are gleaned from study and work and sifted through our sensibilities until, in total, they come to represent why and how we feel, in general, about *performance* and, in particular, what we think of as good or bad. This chapter is one man's siftings. The reader will retain and reject what he needs until, through his own professional life in the musical theater, he defines his own personal ethic. Guglielmo Ferrero, Italian historian and man of letters, in another context said, "What makes good judgment? Experience. What makes experience? Bad judgment."

18

Rideout

But all good things must come to an end, and so one must move forward into the space left by one's conclusions.

—John Ashbery

CLAIMED CONVICTIONS

In the Preface to this volume, I theorize that perhaps there is a tendency to study too much when there is not an ongoing opportunity to work. In my own teaching, when one of my students and I say goodbye to each other, I find myself making a silent prayer that he will forget everything I have taught him. This recollection of Joseph Fuchs, the eminent violinist, of his teacher Franz Kneisel, with whom he had studied from the age of twelve until he was nineteen, is pertinent:

Kneisel said, "You've been with me now almost seven years. You have enough. Go out into the world, do what you can. There's so much I taught you. Remember—if you keep 25 percent it's enough. If you keep 50 percent, it's not as good as 25. If you keep 75, you're in danger. And if you keep 100, then God help you."

(From an interview with Fuchs by Joseph Horowitz, in *The New York Times*, November 11, 1977)

Singing for your supper is the ideal. If consistent opportunity does not present itself, hire a pianist once or twice a month, depending on his availability and the size of your wallet. Buy his time and sing through the songs you want to keep from growing stale—songs you use for auditions and professional engagements. You will be singing and beginning to learn to trust that what you feel and know you are doing well, you *are* doing well. Of course, your criteria will change. They are meant to change. But now your work will be measured, not by a teacher, but against your own idiosyncratic gauge and, most important of all, by audiences.

In the beginning of this decade, the nay-sayers had about buried the musical theater. As late as 1987, when I approached one of our foremost composers to write the preface to *On Performing: A Handbook for Actors, Dancers, and Singers on the Musical Stage,* he countered, without a trace of humor, "What musical stage?" and begged off. He was not alone. Creative artists, producers, critics, and the smart money—everyone, in fact, who had even the smallest fraction of validated input claimed that the musical theater was stagnant, ailing, or just plain dead. (Everyone, that is, except young performers whose need to stand on a stage and sing dies hard. As a teacher in the marketplace and in academia, I can attest to that.) But, as early as January 1988, a glance at the ABC's in the Sunday Arts Section of *The New York Times* listed twenty-one Broadway productions, thirteen of which were musicals and ten of which were superhits; and of the twenty-nine Off-Broadway productions, ten of them were musicals. On the West Coast, touring companies of Broadway hits and pre-Broadway bookings of musicals are still standard procedure, with one Off-Broadway musical the major success story of the Los Angeles theater season. When it makes its promised eastward move, it will not be the first time that a regional production has shifted to New York. True, at this time, there is a rash of English extravaganzas that rake in enormous profits while furthering only the art of the scenic designer but, as I write this, Sondheim is represented, Cole Porter and Kander and Ebb revived, and the curtain still rises and falls on *A Chorus Line.* The truth is that the musical endures. There is, and will always be, something to sing and dance about. One *Fiddler on the Roof* affects and haunts more disparate audiences than any play of the moment; one *Threepenny Opera* sings all we have to know about man's inhumanity to man.

My only concern is for the young performer. We cannot have an artistic musical statement without first-class performances to shape and articulate it. This volume is a byproduct of a new musical theater. It speaks to actors, singers, and dancers—performers, all—who now have less to fear about coming together on the dole than on a stage, but who are not always impelled to raise their work standards sufficiently—to challenge the heritage of an Astaire, a Merman, and a Lahr, among countless others who have gone before. If we are to heed Shakespeare's "What you do still betters what is done," I beg the reader: Continue the climb.

SPEAK WITH DISTINCTION
by Edith Skinner
Revised with New Material by
Timothy Monich and Lilene Mansell

"Edith Skinner's book is the BEST BOOK ON SPEECH THAT I HAVE EVER ENCOUNTERED. It was my primer in school and is my reference book now. To the classical actor, or for that matter any actor who wishes to be understood, this method is a sure guide."
KEVIN KLINE

At last, the "Bible" is back. New chapters and expanded verses join the classic Skinner text to create the authoritative work on American speech for the stage. The long-awaited revised edition of *Speak With Distinction* makes the Skinner Method accessible to all speakers who want to improve their diction. The details of spoken English are examined in a workbook environment, fostering useful voice habits and promoting speech which is efficient, clearly and effortlessly free of regionalisms, appropriate to the dramatic situation, easily articulated, heard and immediately understood in the back rows of a theater.

An **optional 90-minute practice tape** demonstrates the highlights of the Skinner method in six sessions which include examples of all the sounds of Spoken English in isolation, in comparison with each other, and in connected utterance. The tape is accompanied by a **36-page guide to Good Speech** providing a written text of the tape, phonetic notations to help the listener see as well as hear the target sound, tips on how to practice, diagrams and a mini-glossary.

ISBN: 1-55783-047-9

♥APPLAUSE♥